"NATURE AND MEDICINE - TRADITIONAL USES, CHEMISTRY AND BIOPROSPECTING OF NATURAL PRODUCTS"

EDITORS

Dr. Prashith Kekuda T.R. M.Sc., Ph.D.
Assistant Professor, Department of Microbiology,
S.R.N.M.N College of Applied Sciences, N.E.S campu
Balraj Urs road, Shivamogga-577201,
Karnataka, India

Dr. Vinayaka K.S. M.Sc., Ph.D.
Assistant Professor and Head, Department of Botany,
S.V.S College, Bantwal, Dakshina Kannada-574211,
Karnataka, India

Dr. Raghavendra H.L. M.Sc., Ph.D.
Faculty of Medicine, The Medical School (FMB),
Sao Paulo State University (UNESP), Botucatu-18618-687,
Sao Paulo State, Brazil.

ASSOCIATE EDITORS

Dr. Krupanidhi K. M.Sc., Ph.D.
Dr. Sudharshan S.J. M.Sc., Ph.D.
Dr. Archana S. Rao M.Sc., Ph.D.
Dr. Saranraj P. M.Sc., M.Phil., Ph.D.
Ms. Mahalakshmi S.N. M.Sc.

Published by

JPS Scientific Publications
India

Published by

JPS Scientific Publications, Tamil Nadu, India.
E-mail: jpsscientificpublications@gmail.com
Website: www.jpsscientificpublications.com

Published in India.

Editors
Dr. Prashith Kekuda T.R., S.R.N.M.N.C.A.S, Shivamogga, Karnataka, India
Dr. Vinayaka K.S., S.V.S College, Bantwal, Karnataka, India
Dr. Raghavendra H.L., Botucatu, Sao Paulo State, Brazil.

International Standard Book Number (ISBN): 978-81-947154-3-6

JPS Scientific Publications also publishes its books in a variety of Electronic formats. Some content that appears in print may not be available in Electronic formats. For more information visit our publication website www.jpsscientificpublications.com

ABOUT THE EDITORS

Dr. Prashith Kekuda T.R. M.Sc., Ph.D.
Assistant Professor, Department of Microbiology, S.R.N.M.N. College of Applied Sciences, N.E.S. Campus, Balraj Urs Road, Shivamogga-577201, Karnataka, India. Email: prashith_kekuda@rediffmail.com

Dr. Prashith Kekuda T.R. obtained his Master's degree in Microbiology from Kuvempu University, Shivamogga in the year 2002 and Ph.D. degree in Microbiology from the Kuvempu University in the year 2015. He is having an immense experience of 17 years in teaching and 15 ears of research. His research interest includes Microbiology, Lichenology, Phytochemistry, Pharmacology, Bioprospecting of natural sources and Mycology. He has published a number of research and review papers in various reputed National and International journals and authored some book chapters on Biological science. He also served as reviewer for various reputed journals. He has participated in various state, national and international level seminars/conferences/symposia/workshops and presented his research. He is a life member of various organizations such as Indian Lichenological Society, Indian Association of Biomedical Sciences, and Swadeshi Vignana Andolana. Dr. Prashith Kekuda T.R. has guided several research projects for UG and PG students of Microbiology, Botany and Biochemistry. He regularly conducts workshops, seminars, lecture series (invited lectures, career guidance) and quizzes for students on various aspects of biological sciences.

Dr. Raghavendra H.L. M.Sc., Ph.D.
Faculty of Medicine, The Medical School (FMB), Sao Paulo State University (UNESP), Botucatu-18618-687, Sao Paulo State, Brazil. Email: raghu.biogem@gmail.com

Dr. Raghavendra L.S. Hallur has completed his Ph.D in Biochemistry from Kuvempu University, Karnataka, India. Currently, he is serving as FEPESP Postdoctoral Fellow at Botucatu Medical School (FMB), São Paulo State University (UNESP), CEP18618-687 since 2018. Previously, he was serving as Associate Professor of Biochemistry in College of Health Sciences and Publication and Dissemination Director of Wollega University, Nekemte, Ethiopia from 2011-2018. He received 5 Outstanding Presentation award during International Conferences for the best research papers and also awarded 5 times with best employer of Wollega University, Ethiopia. He is a Life Member various scientific societies. He got sanctioned with more than 10 research projects. He published more than 105 articles, organized more than 15 conferences and presented paper in more than 30 national and international conferences. Most importantly he served as Editor in Chief/Editor of Science, Technology and Arts Research Journal (2012-2017), Medical and Health Sciences Research Journal - 2017 and Journal of Agriculture, Food and Natural Resources (2017). He is also serving as Associate Editor BMC Complementary Medicine and Therapies, International Journal of Current Pharmaceutical Research and The Open

Complementary Medicine Journal. His research interests are Phytochemistry, Pharmacology, Diabetes, Oxidative Stress, Bioavailability, Pharmacokinetics, Anticancer Drug Action, Drug Discovery and Delivery and Toxicology.

Dr. Vinayaka K.S. M.Sc., Ph.D.
Assistant Professor and Head, Department of Botany, Sri Venkataramana Swamy College, Vidyagiri, Bantwal-574211, Dakshina Kannada, Karnataka, India. Email: ks.vinayaka@gmail.com

Dr. K.S. Vinayaka is currently working as an Assistant Professor and Head of the Department of Botany, SVS College, Bantwal, Dakshina Kannada, Karnataka, a renowned distinguished academician. He obtained his Ph.D. degree in Botany from the Kuvempu University. Specializing in Ecology and Cryptogammic Botany. He has been teaching and conducting research in Botany for the past one decade. He has working as the head of Botany at SVS College and also served as the Principal of Kumadvathi First Grade College, Shikaripura. His research interest includes Biodiversity, Lichenology, Phytochemistry, Bioprospecting, Plant Taxonomy, Microbiology, Mycology, Ecology, Green energy and Phytomedicine. He has published over 120 research paper in National and International journals and has authored some books on Biological science. He has travelled abroad widely and has presented papers in many international conference and workshops. He has contributed several invited articles to many books and has done extensive research on lichens on which he has published about half dozen papers. He served as the editor of a national level book and is presently working as the editor-in-chief for few national and international level journals. He has received many research awards and grants like DST Young Scientist, Radhakrishna Shikshana Ratna award, SVVS Teaching Excellence Award, Indira Gandhi Sadbhavana award, National Science Foundation (NSF) Travel award, Visiting Scientist grants, Field Museum, USA etc. He was the organizing secretary in National level workshop on Biodiversity and Bioprospecting. He has completed several projects funded by DST, KSTA, VGST, UGC, Rufford, IDEA wild, NSF, MBZ, KFD etc. He also severed as scientific adviser for several NGOs and Committees.

PREFACE

Nature is complete and self-fulfilling in its wholeness. Our forefathers were able to harness the properties of plants, animals and mineral matter to medicate their bodies and to live long and fruitful lives. We have always been passionate about the nature, the source of the medicaments having healing properties. There exists a wealth of information that has been transcribed down from various different cultures across the world. People from most parts of the world rely on medicinal plants for meeting their primary healthcare. According to WHO, 3/4th of population especially living in remote areas depends on medicinal plants as traditional medicine. These natural products have since been harnessed by owners of big Pharma to make medicines for profit. It is well known that a vast majority of drugs available in marked have their origin from natural sources like plants and animals as the leads and the chemistry of most of these drugs have their origin in natural products. Artemisinin, quinine, digoxin, morphine, vincristine and vinblastine are few among the important drugs obtained from natural sources like plants. This book is a collection of chapters that have been written by various authors on different aspects of natural products such as traditional utilization of plants in different localities of India and other parts of the world, chemistry of natural products and screening of natural products for various biological activities. The reader of this book will surely get at least preliminary idea about the role of natural products in human welfare. Moreover, the therapeutic potential of plants mentioned in the chapters may encourage preservation of traditional knowledge on the medicinal properties of the plants. The contributions made by various authors of this book is appreciable. The names of authors has been mentioned in the list of contributors. We thank the associate editors / reviewers for their kind assistance during the review process and for their expert suggestions. Further, we thank the staff of JPS Scientific Publications, Tamil Nadu, India for making every effort to publish this edited book. Special thanks to them for typesetting the entire book and for the production of this book.

Dr. Prashith Kekuda T.R
Dr. Vinayaka K.S
Dr. Raghavendra H.L

LIST OF CONTRIBUTORS

Dr. Archana S. Rao
School of Basic and Applied Sciences, Dayananda Sagar University, Shavige Malleshwara Hills, Kumaraswamy layout, Bangalore-560 111, Karnataka, India.

Dr. Ajay Nair
School of Basic and Applied Sciences, Dayananda Sagar University, Shavige Malleshwara Hills, Kumaraswamy layout, Bangalore-560 111, Karnataka, India.

Dr. Prashith Kekuda T.R.
Department of Microbiology, S.R.N.M.N College of Applied Sciences, N.E.S campus, Balraj Urs road, Shivamogga-577201, Karnataka, India

Dr. Vinayaka K.S.
Assistant Professor and Head, Department of Botany, S.V.S College, Bantwal-574211, Dakshina Kannada, Karnataka, India

Dr. Raghavendra H.L.
Faculty of Medicine, The Medical School (FMB), Sao Paulo State University (UNESP), Botucatu-18618-687, Sao Paulo State, Brazil

Manohara Acharya
Department of Botany, Canara College, Mangaluru-575003, Dakshina Kannada, Karnataka, India

Mahalakshmi S.N.
Department of Zoology, S.R.N.M.N College of Applied Sciences, N.E.S campus, Balraj Urs road, Shivamogga-577201, Karnataka, India

Chaithra M.
Department of Biochemistry, S.R.N.M.N College of Applied Sciences, N.E.S campus, Balraj Urs road, Shivamogga-577201, Karnataka, India

Rithu R.
Department of Microbiology, S.R.N.M.N College of Applied Sciences, N.E.S campus, Balraj Urs road, Shivamogga-577201, Karnataka, India

Rakshitha M.G.
Department of Microbiology, S.R.N.M.N College of Applied Sciences, N.E.S campus, Balraj Urs road, Shivamogga-577201, Karnataka, India

Achala H.G.
P.G. Department of Studies and Research in Biochemistry, Jnana Sahyadri, Kuvempu University, Shankaraghatta-577451, Karnataka, India

Ramyashree K.R.
Division of Biochemistry, J.S.S Academy of Higher Education and Research, Banni Mantap, Mysuru-570015, Karnataka, India

Pramod G.
Department of Microbiology, S.R.N.M.N College of Applied Sciences, N.E.S
campus, Balraj Urs road, Shivamogga-577201, Karnataka, India

Lavanya D.
Department of Microbiology, S.R.N.M.N College of Applied Sciences, N.E.S
campus, Balraj Urs road, Shivamogga-577201, Karnataka, India

Pooja Rao
Department of Microbiology, S.R.N.M.N College of Applied Sciences, N.E.S
campus, Balraj Urs road, Shivamogga-577201, Karnataka, India

Surabhi T.S.
Department of Microbiology, S.R.N.M.N College of Applied Sciences, N.E.S
campus, Balraj Urs road, Shivamogga-577201, Karnataka, India

Soundarya S.
Department of Microbiology, S.R.N.M.N College of Applied Sciences, N.E.S
campus, Balraj Urs road, Shivamogga-577201, Karnataka, India

Fathima Mohammadi
Department of Microbiology, S.R.N.M.N College of Applied Sciences, N.E.S
campus, Balraj Urs road, Shivamogga-577201, Karnataka, India

Shreya K.S.
Department of Microbiology, S.R.N.M.N College of Applied Sciences, N.E.S
campus, Balraj Urs road, Shivamogga-577201, Karnataka, India

Nandini V.
Department of Microbiology, S.R.N.M.N College of Applied Sciences, N.E.S
campus, Balraj Urs road, Shivamogga-577201, Karnataka, India

Supriya H.S.
Department of Microbiology, S.R.N.M.N College of Applied Sciences, N.E.S
campus, Balraj Urs road, Shivamogga-577201, Karnataka, India

Yashaswini S.L.
Department of Microbiology, S.R.N.M.N College of Applied Sciences, N.E.S
campus, Balraj Urs road, Shivamogga-577201, Karnataka, India

Supreetha G.
Department of Microbiology, S.R.N.M.N College of Applied Sciences, N.E.S
campus, Balraj Urs road, Shivamogga-577201, Karnataka, India

Umme Farda Khanum
Department of Microbiology, S.R.N.M.N College of Applied Sciences, N.E.S
campus, Balraj Urs road, Shivamogga-577201, Karnataka, India

Contents

Chapter number	Title	Page number
1	Nature is medicine: Evidence based perspectives Archana S. Rao and Ajay Nair	1 - 10
2	Ethnobotanical survey of Shikaripura taluk, Shivamogga district, Karnataka Vinayaka K.S, Arpitha A.G and Prashith Kekuda T.R.	11 - 29
3	Documentation of Vedic plants of Dakshina Kannada, Karnataka Manohar Acharya	30 - 37
4	An inclusive review on ethnobotanical uses of *Anogeissus latifolia* (Combretaceae) in India Mahalakshmi S.N and Prashith Kekuda T.R.	38 – 50
5	A review on ethnobotanical uses of *Ardisia solanacea* (Poir.) Roxb. (Primulaceae) Rithu R, Rakshitha M.G and Prashith Kekuda T.R*	51 – 59
6	Bioactive compounds from *Alangium salviifolium* (L.f.) Wangerin (Cornaceae) – A mini review. Prashith Kekuda T.R, Mahalakshmi S.N and Chaithra M	60 – 72
7	Elemental analysis and insecticidal activity of leaf and fruit of *Alangium salviifolium* L. (Cornaceae) Lavanya D, Soundarya S, Surabhi T.S, Pooja Rao and Prashith Kekuda T.R	73 – 80
8	*In vitro* antifungal and antiradical activity of Grape seed extract Nandini V, Shreya K.S, Fathima Mohammadi and Prashith Kekuda T.R	81 – 87
9	Ethnoveterinary potential of *Vitex negundo* L. (Lamiaceae) – A review. Prashith Kekuda T.R and Mahalakshmi S.N	88 – 100
10	Antioxidant activity of *Mimusops elengi* L. (Sapotaceae) fruit Ramyashree K.R, Achala H.G, Pramod G and Prashith Kekuda T.R	101 – 111
11	*In vitro* antibacterial activity of fruticose macrolichens of Karnataka, India Vinayaka K.S and Prashith Kekuda T.R	112 – 119
12	Studies on antifungal, antioxidant and insecticidal activities of *Phyllodium pulchellum* (L.) Desv. Supriya H.S, Yashaswini S.L, Supreetha G, Umme Farda Khanum, Prashith Kekuda T.R and Raghavendra H.L	120 – 133

Nature and Medicine: Traditional Uses, Chemistry and Bioprocessing of Natural Products
ISBN: 978-81-947154-3-6
First Edition; 2020
Chapter – 1, Page: 1 - 10

1

NATURE IS MEDICINE: EVIDENCE BASED PERSPECTIVES

Archana S. Rao* and Ajay Nair

School of Basic and Applied Sciences, Dayananda Sagar University, Bengaluru-560111, Karnataka, India

*Corresponding author: archanasrao@dsu.edu.in

Abstract

In this fast pace where life has become a monotonous act of merely getting through one's daily routine, unwanted stress, unhealthy food and an overall pessimism has made life complicated and unhappy. Therefore, to achieve goals, having a meaningful life demands an equal serving of the physical, mental, and spiritual wellbeing. This is because health, at all these levels is interconnected. Unfortunately, man's obsession towards a dominion over this planet has in turn brought about his own downfall, where he has completely disconnected himself from nature. By restricting himself and keeping away from nature, man has become his own aspiring god, forgetting the fact that he too is a part of it. Mother earth nurtures every living being and teaches it how to survive. Nature has answers to one's welfare that needs to be sought for by human beings. This chapter summates several instances on how nature itself is the medicine for all the diseases and disorders contributing towards health and longevity.

Key words: Nature, Medicine, Behavior, Animals, Vedas, Simple life and Ayurveda.

1. Introduction

Life on earth as we know it, began with complete awareness of the surroundings. In other words, a constant, undying interaction between matter and energy engendered what we call life. From elemental states such as atoms and molecules, to more complex states such as cells, tissues, or the whole organism, all are conscious of their bearings on earth. By adapting against an ever-changing surrounding, the organisms evolved for survival and perpetuation. And optimal survival bred competition that never wanes. During this constant struggle for continuance, every living individual would coevolve with one other (positively or negatively) as put admirably by Sir Charles Darwin in his masterpiece, 'On the Origin of Species'.

As we all know, human beings are considered to be one of the more evolved species. However, this realization has made us believe as though we own this planet. We are not gate-keepers; all that intellectual control is too tempting to give up. But not so long ago our anthropological ancestors shared an eco-friendlier view. Be it hunters, who never killed more than they ate, or planters who never cultivated more than they inhabited. To them they were one among the several beings who walked upon this earth. If we were to remove all human beings from the face of this planet, it would still go on cycling under all the fixed laws that govern it. But if we remove microorganisms from earth, that surely will have a devastating impact.

If we start listing the effects microbes have both (beneficial and detrimental), the list will go on tirelessly. In the recent past, host-pathogen interactions, has been the cornerstone for research on understanding disease pathophysiology. Host-pathogen interactions are strongly under the influence of natural selection (Duxbury *et al.*, 2019). Pathogens evolve with their host and thus susceptibility or resistance to a particular disease is always decided by both host and pathogen. Nature is unbiased! It always, be it pathogen or the host, selects and promotes the best available alternate.

When we look at the current scenario worldwide, the infectious diseases are emerging and re-emerging. These infectious diseases caused by various groups of microorganisms are having impact not only on the physical health of individuals but also on the socio-economics, life style and mental status. Treatment of infectious and other non-infectious diseases mainly relay on allopathic medical interventions. Allopathic drugs for the most part focus more on subsiding the superficial symptom rather than treating the root cause. The antibiotics against infectious diseases are not specific to the infectious agent alone, but also affects the natural microbiota of our

body. This when combined with the several associated side-effects that accompany allopathy, outweighs any positive therapeutic effect it might have.

If one is to evaluate why modern drugs fail with a fair share of adverse drug reactions that each drug carries, one has to first look at the underlying principle that governs any present-day drug designing. All drug designing is premised upon a lock and key mechanism. If the drug target or pathogen is akin to a lock, then the drug is analogous to a key. With a proper key, one aims at opening the lock. But this strategy only holds true in an ideal world where one has an unchanging lock. It does not accommodate evolutionary change which is the one true constant in the biological world. So as pathogens or biological drug targets are under the constant selective pressure, they change at rates beyond the limited permutation and combination, drug designing methods account for. And with this, one eventually ends with a drug which either fails, or is incapable of being specific.

Whatever we create mimicking nature cannot be an exact replicate. For example, penicillin manufactured synthetically is nowhere comparable to the penicillin produced by *Penicillium* sp. naturally. Every drug developed fails – as a result resistance builds up, because the pathogen is in continuous race against natural selection to be better than the host, and vice-versa evolving naturally against the challenges. For them it is survival strategies. For example, a deer that is chased by a tiger, evolved to run faster with a larger heart and long legs. On the other hand, the tiger evolved with traits such as keen hearing, camouflage, and ambush hunting. Therefore, it is imperative that one looks out for other alternatives to treat both infectious and non-infectious diseases. Co-evolution conceptually, shows that the solution exists in nature itself. Human body is highly evolved in several ways in particularly with a strong immunity. The natural healing techniques are always safe and perhaps the best way to get rid of ailments. The human body is composed of trillions of cells. The microbiome of human body dominates these cells and has a definitive impact on our body, mind and activities. Hence the measures taken to treat human body should be holistic, focusing on not disturbing the natural abilities but to enhance it.

2. The Vedic Way of Life

"Vedic Way of Life" is not just a mode or part of life or ritual practices. It is a scientific philosophy based on years of research and understanding the nuances of nature. One of its greatest philosophies talks about how every action of ours will have a definitive impact on our lives and also on the nature.

Vedic scriptures mention many concepts existing in modern microbiology. The vedic approaches towards healing and curing diseases were holistic. "Disease" that is, dis- ease indicates discomfort of the body. The vedic methods of treating diseases are comprehensive. As it works at different levels – physical, mental and spiritual. Whole world accepted the vedic way of greeting by joining hands together, rather than shaking hands. Similarly, several vedic concepts have now caught everyone's attention in the scientific community. Many researches are going on across the globe to test the vedic concepts and vedic way of medicine.

Traditional Medicine describes extensively on the historical use of herbs for many ailments. Ayurveda is a science, researched and has an history of nearly 5000 years. Yoga is a not only mere physical activity. It is again a science to train the mind and body. The traditional ways to treat any diseases or impairments are to create a balance between the food, medicine and physical body. Hence any traditional medicine includes both diet and herbal medicine giving equal importance to body, mind and spirit in treating or preventing diseases. Many plants which were life saviors are now extinct.

Yoga is a practice which not only trains the physical body, but balances the physiology. Pranayama helps in breathing and makes sure each and every cell gets enough oxygen. Whole body gets rejuvenated and energized. The yogic diet is carefully designed based on the careful understanding of the nature. At emotional and spiritual levels, yoga and meditation elevates the individual and makes him realise the eternal bliss. Yoga is not a part or practice of life. It is "a way of life" (Shekhar, 2016).

Suśrutasaṃhitā, a Vedic literature states sun as giver and sustainer of life. In Matsya Purana sun is depicted as"Aarogyam Bhashkaradichhet", giver of good health. Surya Namaskara is crafted based on such concepts, which balances the body and brings the individual in harmony with nature. Rig Veda also quotes sun which heals cardiac diseases, jaundice, anemia etc. Atharva Veda enlists treating 22 diseases including lungs, eye, bones, tuberculosis, wounds, knees, thighs, heart problems and anemia etc. using sunlight. Sun prolongs life and eases from diseases at mental, physical and spiritual levels.

The festivals celebrated in India and practices attached to each one of them, we can see reason, each relates to the seasonal variations of nature. The foods suggested for each festival makes sense scientifically. This is a simple example to show how our lives were beautifully carved by our ancestors, in tune with nature. The modern life styles are not giving rooms to synchronize our living harmoniously with nature.

The practices like homa, mentioned in vedic texts have various benefits. Yagna is not mere burning of woods. If we try to reason it scientifically, rather than see it as a meagre ritual practice, one can understand the importance of it. Daily yagna in the form of Agnihotra was prescribed in ancient texts. It purifies air, kills microbes in air, positively impacts on respiration.

Vedic microbiology, clearly explains germ theory of diseases. Form, how to treat the diseases naturally by using herbs, yagna technique, cow dung, cow urine, ghee etc. As it is well established, products from cow are treated as holy, because of their benefits on human health (Frend, 2018).

3. Anda – Brahmanda: Microcosm - Macrocosm

The unity between microcosm and macrocosm, which is known as pindanda – brhmanda in vedic texts – speaks about the underlying unity between two. That is very clear that the awareness of one's self.

यत् पिण्डे तत् ब्रह्माण्डे ।

That means macrocosm within the microcosm. That means, you are a universe within the universe, you are made up of the elements of universe and you are a miniature universe. To be more precise you are a part of nature. And also implies use nature's own properties to balance the microcosmic body.

At spiritual level, our self-consciousness is part of a universal consciousness. At mental level, it is awareness of self and connection with universe and at physical level, we are made up of universal elements, atoms and molecules. Hence we are indistinguishable from nature. We are building barriers at all 3 levels, and that makes us feel disconnected. But the ultimate truth has to be accepted.

If you start knowing your own self, then the realization of one-ness with nature is obvious. We are all just matter co-existing with energy. Even Einstein in his monumental work on special relativity beautifully articulated that matter and energy are not absolute, they are interconvertible. The entire ayurvedic concepts are based on this aspect. Single cell microorganisms and multi-cellular organisms are made up of these 5 elements. These elements are ubiquitous and constitutes all life forms, by combining in various ways (Pawan Kumar, 2016).

4. Simple Living

Since his inception man has been living alongside nature. Therefore, all the evolutionary memory accumulated is conserved and has been inadvertently passed on in every generation. The artificial environments created by man unfortunately

breaks this evolutionary link, goes against nature and leads to a series of complications that then need to be solved with synthetic drugs.

Nature provides sustenance to all beings. The pressure created by nature forces every living being to evolve or perish. Nature has solution to everything. If you peep into mother's kitchen, one finds medicine for simple health problems like acidity to more complex diseases like cancer. Plants offer us solutions from pimples to wrinkles. All the medicines we require is available in nature. But we have barely scratched the surface. Nature offers free access to her medicinal marvels, however how far we explore is up to us. There are simple ways of living. Simple solutions to turning life into healthy living. Being aware of one's self, what we eat and the lifestyle is paramount.

If we have any diseases or health issues, first we have to be aware of what is happening to the body. Then ask the mind to stay calm, not making it to sound complicated. Then mind can guide body to react accordingly. Body listens to mind, and mind should understand the body. This self-realization on body-mind coordination is the simplest solution for most complicated problems. When young, our brains were active, grasping and gathering every small detail. As we grow, our minds got conditioned making us think only in particular directions. But why? Because as children we were far more ignorant. Ignorance breeds curiosity, and an openness towards everything we experience. To explore the true potential nature holds, we need to first embrace that whatever we call science yet, is accumulated memory. To know further, one needs to continue seeking with an all accepting ignorant mind. Simple solutions are not easily acceptable by people because of the conditioning of mind. As a matter of fact, the success story of human evolution has premised upon on one evolutionary trait: willingness to experiment and learn. A trait forsaken long ago.

Why we feel when we go out for a walk, or go to a beach and see sunset, go for a trek and enjoy the breeze, just sit on bank of river and enjoy the sky above, why we stare at night sky glowing with stars and moon. Keeping ourselves closer to nature is always joyful, gives happiness, peace and health. All of us have evolutionary memory. Every organism has evolutionary adaptations that they developed by living in a total natural environment for years. Theory of Biophilia (Wilson, 1984). According to the theory of biophilia, the modern brain is inherited product of evolution of a brain which was inured to extract, process and evaluate the information from nature (Wilson, 1984; 1993). The brain evolved in a biocentric world, not a machine regulated world.

Research has shown that natural sounds, sights, smell directly impacts stress in a positive way. These natural aspects affect blood pressure and even hormonal biomarkers of stress such as the levels of cortisol in blood. Many researches are going on to treat diseases and disorders by treatments like music therapy, color therapy,

dance therapy, aroma therapy, vibronics etc. Again and again these concepts prove the natural way of healing as the best.

The genetic material consisting of introns and exons, gives clues to the preserved memories. Though introns are considered junk DNA, they are retained and continued to inherit through generations. Nature never thought of discarding them considering, the energy spent to replicate and maintain them when eventually they get spliced out from coding mRNA. But evolution preserved a lot of memories in these introns. Since the sequencing of the human genome, it became apparent that one cannot simply explain inheritance from a protein-centric world. The non-coding DNA, of which introns are also part of account for roughly 95 % of the human genome. And this so-called junk DNA is what validates the existence of the meager 5 %, i.e., the manifested inheritance (Nair and Rao, 2020).

Epipsychology is a recent branch of study which deals with the psychological, emotional relationships with the natural world. The theory clearly speaks that the man's relationship with nature is not only physical but also mental and emotional (Jordan *et al.,* 2010). Interface of ecology and psychology, philosophy of environments.

5. Clues from the Wild Life

Careful observation of wild life gives us many clues in this regard. How wild animals fight infections? How plants build up self defense mechanisms and fights against pathogens and at the same time how infectious agents find new ways for their living?

Animals in wild are best examples for proving Nature is Medicine. Animals show many behavioral responses towards infectious diseases. They avoid diseases by removing parasites. Removing ticks, lice and fleas are commonly seen in arthropods (Hart, 1997). Many animals exhibit fly-repelling behavior by tail switching, muscle flicking, stamping legs etc. (Hart, 2011). They eliminate many feeding sites, especially to avoid faeces so that to avoid intestinal parasites (Taylor, 1954; Odberg, 1977). Many animals prefer not to eat dead animals, but eat only those who die by hunting by themselves. Few animals eat dead animals even though they were infected, because most infections are species specific (Fox, 1975).

Licking the wounds is observed in many animals as saliva contains lysozyme, lactoferrin, leucocytes, lactoperoxidase and immunoglobulins etc. (Bowen, 1974; Mandel, 1987) and growth factors (Dagogo-Jack *et al.,* 1985; Petrides *et al.,* 1984). Dog's saliva is found to be bactericidal (Hart and Powell, 1990).

Quarantine has become a household name since the onset of the COVID-19 pandemic. However, several animals have been using it as a strategy to the spreading of infections. Territorial defense is commonly seen in primates (Altmann and Altmann, 1970; Freelan, 1976). Animals are very well aware of prophylactic and

therapeutic herbs, and they prefer the formal. Cats and dogs eat plants to eliminate their parasite loads in intestine (Sueda *et al.,* 2008). Concept of prebiotics was observed in chimpanzees. By eating leaves which cannot be digested, they increase intestinal motility and eliminate parasites. (Huffman and Caton, 2001).

Therapeutic use of herbs is rarely seen, chimpanzee which chew bitter pith of *Vernonina* sp. for antimicrobial activity when sick (Huffman and Seifu, 1989). As with quarantine, immune-priming behaviours that play a role in disease protection can also be important for introducing the young to real food, protection of food resources and maintaining good nesting sites (Hart, 2011). Animals take care of the injured and sick (Douglas-Hamilton *et al.,* 2006).

Humans were also once living in wild, and had all these inherent qualities to live in compliance with nature. Getting back to such root concepts, acquiring hints from wild life to find the missing links to regain the relationship with nature is need of the hour.

6. Conclusion

In the past few decades, our life's have become so regimented that, for reasons unknown, for every concern be it physical or mental, we resort to solutions that are documented via limited research. Common sense or logic has apparently taken a back seat. Sophisticated solutions make more sense than simple ones. We seem to always undervalue the importance of just taking a walk in the sun or a beach when mentally unwell. However, when the same suggestion comes from a doctor, who might suggest that along with a prescription medicine, it all seems to fall in place. These innate responses from and to nature have always been an integral part of our cultural history. But yet, we are nowhere close to realizing the infinite medicinal solutions nature encompasses. But there is a silver lining nonetheless. Gradually and substantially, the multitude healing properties of nature is getting apparent, and being introduced in the health-care systems around the globe. Japan, for example, has introduced what they call as 'Forest Therapy Centers' that is being used by hospitals, NGOs to help people cope with several ailments, both physical and mental. The vedic practices, traditional methods, Ayurveda and other alternate medicines are now again coming into the main stream for health care. Now having said this, we don't necessarily need to institutionalize ourselves to recognize nature and its inherent medicinal benefits. But for now, having a prescribed route would certainly program the coming generation to think of it as a more potent option than pharmaceutical approach that either works with side effects or doesn't work at all.

7. References

1) Altmann SA, Altmann J. Baboon ecology: African field research. Chicago, IL: University of Chicago Press, 1970.

2) Bowen WH. Defense mechanisms in the mouth and their possible role in the prevention of dental caries: a review. Journal of Oral Pathology 1974; 3: 266–278.

3) Dagogo-Jack S, Atkinson S, Kendall-Taylor P. Homologous radioimmunology for epidermal growth factor in human saliva. Journal of Immunoassay 1985; 6: 125–136.

4) Douglas-Hamilton I, Bhalla S, Wittemyer G, Vollrath F. Behavioural reactions of elephants towards a dying and deceased matriarch. Applied Animal Behaviour Sciences 2006; 100: 87–102.

5) Duxbury EML, Day JP, Vespasiani M, Thuringer Y, Sophia IT, Smith CL, Tagliaferri L, Kamacioglu A, Lindsley I, Love L, Unkless RL, Jiggins FM, Longdon B. Host-pathogen coevolution increases genetic variation in susceptibility to infection. eLIFE 2019; 8: e46440.

6) Fox LR. Cannibalism in natural populations. Annual Reviews of Ecological Systematics 1975; 6: 719–728.

7) Freeland W J. Pathogens and the evolution of primate sociality. Biotropica 1976; 8: 12–24.

8) Frend C. Vedic Microbiology: Microbiology in the Vedas – A revived history. In. Vedic Science 2018; 8(4): 27-34.

9) Hart BL. Behavioural defence. In Host–parasite evolution: general principles and avian models (eds Clayton D. H., Moore J.), Oxford, UK: Oxford University Press, 1997, pp. 59–77.

10) Hart BL. Behavioural defences in animals against pathogens and parasites: parallels with the pillars of medicine in humans. Philosophical transactions of the Royal Society of London. Series B, Biological sciences 2011; 366(1583), 3406–3417.

11) Hart BL, Powell K. Antibacterial properties of saliva: role in maternal periparturient grooming and in licking wounds. Physiology and Behaviour 1990; 48, 383–386.

12) Huffman MA, Caton JM. Self-induced increase of gut motility and the control of parasitic infections in wild chimpanzees. Internat. Journal of Primatology 2001; 22: 329–346.

13) Huffman MA, Seifu M. Observations on the illness and consumption of a possibly medicinal plant, Vernonia amygdalina (Del.), by a wild chimpanzee in the Mahale Mountains National Park, Tanzania. Primates 1989; 30: 51–63.

14) Jordan M, Stevens, P, Milton M. Ecopsychology: Past, present and future. European Journal of Ecopsychology 2010; 1: 1-3.

15) Mandel JD. The functions of saliva. Journal of Dental Research 1987; 66: 623–627.

16) Nair A, Rao AS. The silence eclipsing introns. Japanese Journal of Gastroenterology and Hepatology 2020; 4(14): 1-3.

17) Odberg FO, Francis-Smith K. Studies on the formation of ungrazed eliminative areas in fields used by horses. Applied Animal Ethology 1977; 3: 27–34.

18) Petrides PE, Bfhlen P, Shivley JE. Chemical characterization of the two forms of epidermal growth factor in murine saliva. Biochemical and Biophysical Research Communications 1984; 125: 218–228.

19) Shekhar TV. Yogasanjeevini. The Elixir of Life. Lathashekhar. 2016, 21-31.

20) Sueda KLC, Hart BL, Cliff KD. Characterisation of plant eating in dogs. Applied Animal Behavior Science 2008; 111: 120–132.

21) Taylor RJ. Grazing behavior and helmintic disease. British Journal of Animal Behavior 1954; 2: 61–62.

22) Wilson EO. Biophilia. Harvard University Press, Massachusetts, 1984.

23) Wilson EO. Biophilia. Cambridge: Harvard University Press, 1984.

24) Wilson EO. 'Biophilia and the conservation ethic', in S.R. Kellert and E.O. Wilson (eds.), The Biophilia Hypothesis (Island Press, Washington DC), 1993, Pp. 31–41.

Cite this chapter as:

Rao AS, Nair A. Nature is medicine: Evidence based perspectives. In: Kekuda PTR, Vinayaka KS, Raghavendra HL (Editors), Nature and Medicine: Traditional uses, chemistry and bioprospecting of natural products. JPS Scientific Publications, Tamil Nadu, India, 2020, Pp 01 - 10.

Nature and Medicine: Traditional Uses, Chemistry and Bioprocessing of Natural Products
ISBN: 978-81-947154-3-6
First Edition; 2020
Chapter – 2, Page: 11 - 29

2

ETHNOBOTANICAL SURVEY OF SHIKARIPURA TALUK, SHIVAMOGGA DISTRICT, KARNATAKA, INDIA

Vinayaka K. S[1]*, Arpitha A. G[2] and Prashith Kekuda T. R[3]

[1]Plant Biology Lab, Department of Botany, Sri Venkatramana Swamy College, Vidyagiri, Bantwal, Dakshina Kannada, Karnataka, India

[2]Department of Botany, Kumadvathi First Grade College, Shikaripura, Shivamogga, Karnataka, India

[3]Department of Microbiology, S.R.N.M.N College of Applied Sciences, Balraj Urs road, Shivamogga, Karnataka, India

*Corresponding author: ks.vinayaka@gmail.com

Abstract

The use of medicinal plants in the treatment and prevention of diseases is attracting the attention of scientists worldwide. The specific part of the plant used for medicinal applications varies from species to species and from one traditional healer to another. This study was carried out to explore and record those plants and plant parts used for treating various human and veterinary ailments by the healers of Shikaripura taluk. Ethnobotanical data were collected from 16 traditional healers (13 males and 3 females) in the taluk, by a data capture questionnaire focusing on the local names of the medicinal plants , their medicinal uses, the plant parts used, and methods of preparation and of administering treatments to patients. The present survey identified 144 medicinal plants from 22 families, with 128 genera, used to treat a various range of ailments in the Shikaripura taluk. The Apocyanaceae family

was the most commonly used family representing 43 % of all the medicinal plant species recorded by this study, followed by the Fabaceae at 19 %. The plant parts most frequently used were the roots (44 %), followed by the leaves (26 %), bark (15 %), the whole plant (11 %), and flowers and fruits (4 %). Most of the traditional healers obtained their extracts by boiling the medicinal plants. The most often recurring ailments treated by healers was stomach problems for both human and veterinary ailments, using 31 % of all medicinal plants reported in this study for preparing such treatments. The following medicinal plants were the most common plants covered by this study were *Achyranthes aspera, Calotropis gigantia, Abrus pricatorius, Curcuma domestica, Plumbago zeylanica, Tabernaemontana alternifolia* and *Azardirachta indica.* The rural communities of the Shikaripura taluk possess a wealth of information on medicinal plants and their applications. This ethnobotanical survey can help scientists identify for further research those plants whose medicinal properties may be useful in the development of new drugs.

Key words: Ethnobotany, Traditional healers, Ayurveda, Shikaripura

1. Introduction

Today ethnobotany has become an important and crucial area of research and development, sustainable utilization of bioresource management and socio-economic development is very important aspect (Jouad *et al.*, 2001). Nowadays, the botanists, social scientists, anthropologists, the practitioners of indigenous medicines all over the world are engaged in the study of man-plant interactions in a natural environment (Dhiman *et al.*, 2008). As plants become very useful for herbals and their economic value increased. The important and possible benefit of plant-based medicines constitutes a rewarding in the area of research and development, particularly in developing countries like India which is having a rich biodiversity of plant resources and they are coupled with a high prevalence and severity of infectious spreading diseases (Usmane *et al.*, 2016). The indigenous people of different regions have been developed their own way of utilization of medicinal plants for their health benefits and following their traditional culture and customs (Rajkumar and Shivanna, 2009). The knowledge is orally transferred from one generation to another (Rajkumar and Shivanna, 2009).

The traditional medicine still has remained as the most affordable commodity and very easily accessible source of treatment to the primary healthcare system rural communities of India. The tribal's depend mostly on forest flora for meeting their day today needs and primary health care. The primitive societies in India have been dependent on herbal medicines the time immemorial (Nair, 1999). About 5000 plant species have been recorded so far which are used by tribals and aboriginal communities in different states (Jha, 2001). Ethnobotany is a rapidly developing

science, it well catching people with varying range of academic background and curiosity. It is still dominantly linked with the potential utilization and economic value of various plants. There is an intimate connection to the life of an explore and the promise of finding gold in the form of plants as potential bioresource for life saving drugs that could become important in the treatment of various diseases like Cancer and AIDS also. The indigenous knowledge of the veterinary health care system acquired by traditional herbal healers is orally transformed from one generation to other. The rich and diversified flora of India provides valuable storehouse of medicinal plants (Ohemu *et al.*, 2014). Many herbs and minerals used in Ayurveda were described by ancient Indian herbalists such as Charak and Shushruta (Ahma *et al.*, 2017). Due to lack of interest among the younger generation as well as their tendency to migrate to cities for lucrative jobs, most of the traditional knowledge had faded away and there is a possibility of losing the existing knowledge totally in the near future (Suresh *et al.*, 2018). The main focus of the present study is to ascertain the detailed information on the use of plants and their therapeutic medical practices among rural areas of Shikaripura taluk of Shivamogga district, Karnataka.

2. Methodology

Study Area

We have selected Shikaripura taluk of Shivamogga district, Karnataka as our study area. Shikaripura taluk starts from the foot hills of centre parts of Western Ghats to the Eastern plans and it lies between 14°16′N to 14°27′N and 75°21′ E to 75°35′ E with an average altitude of 603MSL to 980MSL. It includes semi-evergreen and deciduous type of forest. It lies between plane land of bayaluseme and tropical forest of malenadu. Field survey was conducted in various localities of the taluk such as Togarsi, Kowli, Yelgere, Salur, Mallur, Shiralkoppa, Balligavi, Ambligolla, Tarlghatta, Marvallithanda, Esur, Udagani, Tadagani, Punedahalli, Belvanthanakoppa, Bhadrapura and Yelaneerkoppa. An initial survey of village population indicated that they use home remedies which in practical terms mean that such remedies are being used without consultation with any traditional medicinal practitioner.

The list of herbal healers residing in the study area was prepared by gathering the information from the local people and some local agencies. Before going to the field work, a rapport should be established with the well-known persons of the particular visiting village, as the selection of informants form a very important aspect of ethnobotanical study in the field. Experienced people such as herbal healers, bone-setters, birth attendants, shepherds, head-man and well knowledgeable senior people

of the study locality were contacted for collecting the information on their knowledge of medicinal valuable plants for treating various human and veterinary diseases.

The knowledge of rural communities about plants in near to them and their usage were studied by own observation and interrogation. Schultes (1963) opined that "Perhaps the most satisfying way of studying ethnobotany is the direct investigation among primitive people. In so far as this is time consuming, it is not easy, but it cannot be called difficult and hazardous". Hence, the above said approach was employed for documenting the people's knowledge of medicinal plants. The common requirements of field work were contact with informants, procurement of information, collection of voucher specimens, and identification, and evaluation of information

Requirements for Field study

The materials required for the collection of ethnobotanical data and preparing herbarium specimens are as follows:

a) Field note book, pencil and pen
b) Tape recorder and camera
c) Secateur, knife and digger
d) Polythene bags
e) Plant pressing board for preparing voucher specimens
f) Blotter sheets and news papers
g) Pocket lens (10x)

An Ethno-medico-botanical survey was conducted during August 2018 to March 2019 in selected villages in Shikaripura taluk of Shivamogga district. Surveys were conducted in 16 selected villages in Shikaripura for identifying herbal practitioners and to collect herbal knowledge. The ethnomedico-botanical data were collected through interviews and discussion with village herbal practitioners and knowledgeable elder people of different communities resident in the study area using the questionnaire designed by Sinha (1996). During the study some major herbal practitioner was contacted for adequate information on plant species and their medicinal uses with reference of few special diseases. The ethno medicinal information of plants was also collected through different techniques such as open ended, interview question was of semi-structured and structured types one (Martin, 1995; Cotton, 1997).

During our field visits information on sex, level of education, age, religion, ethnicity and occupation of informants were collected, vernacular names of plants and their growth form, abundance, parts used for medicine, storage method,

methods of remedy preparation, dosage prescriptions for each disease, mode of remedy given, other uses of the each medicinal plant species and their threats to those medicinal plant species and their local conservation practices methods were collected. The information collected was confirmed by discussion with respondents those who received herbal treatments form a particular practicenar. Data were cross checked and they were compared with the already existing literature like (Jain, 1991; Kirtikar and Basu, 1995; Maheshwari et al, 1993). During our survey, local names of plant specimens were confirmed by showing live plant specimens to traditional practiceners of the local region. Plants species were identified and confirmed by using the standard floras (Ramaswamy et al, 2001; Gamble, 1995; Yoganarasimhan et al, 1981; Saldanha and Nicolson, 1976). Voucher specimens were photographed for future study.

Figure 1: Map of Shikaripura taluk showing study area

Interview Techniques

The main method of gathering ethnobotanical information was to talk/discuss with people, to watch what they do and to participate in their activities. During the field survey, ethnobotanical information was collected by interview techniques as described by Martin (1995) and Alexiades (1996). The open ended interview had no structure, but involves simply making notes during or after the casual conversation. Many insights that were obtained during casual conversations were recorded with an audio tape recorder. Many of the plants reported during interviews were located and collected from different vegetation zones during the field visit undertaken along with informants. In Semi-structured interview, a list of questions and topics that need to be covered were prepared, but this list was only a guideline which allowed good flexibility. During discussion, new lines of inquiry that might arise naturally if any, was also documented. Data analyses were done by using standard formulas.

3. Results and Discussion

A total of sixteen respondents were recorded in the study area (13 male and 3 female individuals) they were belongs to different castes and communities. Majority of resident herbal healers consider their medicinal care knowledge as traditional their secrets, but very rarely revealed their knowledge upon repeated visits and questions. They were also informed of the importance of medicinal value to human beings. The present survey revealed the information on the usage of 144 plant species that have capacity to cure human and animal ailments (Table 1 and 2). Among them 42 were herbs, 16 were climbers, 34 were shrubs and 52 were tress species.

Table - 1: Plant species use to treat human diseases and their formulations

Vernacular name	Botanical name	Family	Diseases	Part used	Method used
Lolesara	*Aloe vera* (L.) Burm.f.	Liliaceae	Itching	Leaves	*Aloe* with honey, cloves and piper
Uttarani	*Achyranthes aspera* L.	Amaranthaceae	Gastric problem	Root	root juice were given for oral
Maddale	*Alstonia scholaris* (L.) R.Br.	Apocynaceae	Fever	Bark	One Handful of bark is taken with rice water orally
Nelabevu	*Andrographis panicaluata* (Burm.F.) Nees	Acanthcea	Itching	Leaves	Juice of leaves taken orally
Bevu	*Azadirachta indica* A. Juss	Meliaceae	Body ache	Leaves	One handful of leaves boiled in 4 lit. of water and made into decoction

Bellulli	*Allium sativum* L.	Lilliaceae	Ear ache	Bulb	Boil four loaves of garlic in water, smash them and pinch of salt. woolen cloth and placed in aching ear.
Honagone	*Alternanthera sessilis* (L.) R.Br.ex DC	Amaranthace	Stomach ache	Leaves	1/2kg leaves fried in gee. Taken orally
Bilvapatre	*Aegle marmelos* (L.) Correa.	Rutaceae	Asthma	Leaves	1kg Of leaves boiled in 4L Of water and made decoction and taken orally.
Surya kanthi soppu	*Anagallis arvensis* L.	Primulaceae	Ulcers	Leaf	Paste of leaves is applied on wounds and ulcers
Erulli	*Allium cepa* L.	Liliaceae	Blood pressure	Bulb	Infusion of leaves of brahmi, flowers of night jasmine and onion bulb taken.
Basale soppu	*Basale alba* L.	Basellaceae	Mouth ulcer	Leaf	Orally taken every day (leaves are chewed)
Kiri brahmi	*Bacopa monieri* (Linn.)Pennell	Scrophulariaceae	Hair fall, fungal growth	Seeds	Seed oil extracted is applied as antiseptic to check fungal growth on head and inhabits hair fall
Talemara	*Boerhaavia diffusa* (L.)	Areaceae	Leucorrhoea	Whole plant	Decoction of plant given once a day in the early morning
Muttugada	*Butea monosperma* (Lam.)	Fabaceae	Urinary injection	Bark	One cup of bark decoction is taken orally.
Kurtigana soppu	*Capparis zeylanica* L.	Capparaceae	Cough and cold	Leaves	Leaf juice mixed with a cup of fresh goat's milk orally
Bekkina budde gida	*Cardiospermum halicacabum* L.	Sapindaceae	Cough	Leaves	A handful of fresh leaves smoke is inhaled
Kavalu	*Careya arborea* Roxb.	Lecythidaceae	Dysentery	Bark	One teaspoon full of bark taken with a cow milk orally
Tea soppu	*Camellia sinensis* (L.) Kuntze	Theaceae	Dysentery	Leaves	Boiled in water. Lemon and pepper is added, drink for 2-3 times a day

Ekka	*Calatropis procera* (Aiton) R.Br	Asclepiadaceae	Snake bite	Root barks milk latex.	Root barks paste given orally to patients, to induce vomiting and later applied over the bitten area
Kakke mara	*Cassia fistula* L.	Caesalpiniaceae	Acidity, headache, wounds jaundice	Leaves	A hand full of leaves boiled in six liters of water and reduced to one liter decoction and taken orally with cow milk.
Nithya kanagala	*Catharanthus roseus* (L.) G.Don	Apocynaceae	Blood pressure	Leaves	About 5-6 leaves chewed and juice is taken daily
Ondelaga	*Centella asiatica* (L.) Urb.	Apiaceae	Fever, cardiac problem	Leaves, roots	Leaf paste of Ondelaga and Bilva is taken orally
Ballivadaka	*Clematis gouriana* Roxb.Ex DC.	Ranunculaceae	Headache	Stem, Leaves	Pieces of stem (or) a handful of leaves are boiled in water and vapor is inhaled.
Jeerige	*Cuminum cyminum* L.	Apiaceae	Body heat	Seeds	Seeds crushed with sugar candy and mixed with coconut milk taken orally
Arishina	*Curcuma longa* L.	Zingiberaceae	Scabies	Rhizome	Rhizome crushed with cumin seeds and made into paste, which is applied externally on affected part.
Thengu	*Cocos nucifera* L.	Arecaceae	Stomach pain, wrinkles	Fruit	Cardamom fruits and copra are mixed in sugar and eaten.
Paccha karpura	*Cinnamomum camphora* (L.) Nees.	Lauraceae	Wounds	Leaves	Paste of leaves and camphor is used to affected area.
Nimbe	*Citrus medica* var. *acida* Brandis	Rutaceae	Acidity	Fruit	Infusion of wild tobacco root is prepared along with lemon juice and it's to be applied on affected region.

Limbu	*Citrus aurantifolia* (Chritm).	Rutaceae	Itching	Fruit	Squeeze out a little lemon juice over itchy area.
Dalchinni	*Cinnamomum zeylanicum* Bl.	Lauraceae	Itching	Leaves	Powdered leaves are used affected area.
Southe kayi	*Cucumis sativus* L.	Cucurbitaceae	Dry chopped lips	Fruit	Cut fine slice of cucumber and rub on lips thin slice are kept on eyes to remove dark circles
Agalashuntib alli	*Cyclea peltata* (Lam.) Hook.f. and Thomson	Menisperm aceae	Dysentery, intestinal Worms	Leaves	One tea spoon of leaf is taken orally
Garike	*Cynodon dactylon* (L.) pers.	Poaceae	Dandruff, fever	Leaf	Leaf paste applied to wound
Ragi	*Eleusine coracana* (L.) Gaertn.	Poaceae	Body cooling	Seeds	Seeds are cooked in water and grind with jaggery.
Nilagiri mara	*Eucalyptus tereticornis* Sm.	Myrtaceae	Head ache	Leaves	Applied oil to pain part of the body
Engu/Hingu	*Ferula assafoetida* L.	Apiaceae	Stomach ache	Crystalline root	Leaf paste is applied on tooth.
Atti hannu	*Ficus recemosa* (L.)	Moraceae	Leucorrhea/piles	Fruit	100gm of cumin seeds and 1tsp full of paste is taken orally with 1/2Tsp of gee. Bark powder is taken orally
Aralimara	*Ficus religiosa* L.	Moraceae	Skin allergies	Bark	Bark powder paste is applied externally
Gobbarada gida	*Gliricidia sepium* (Jacq.) Walp.	Papilionaceae	Ring worm	Leaves	Leaves paste is applied externally over ring worm part
Jesta madhu	*Glycyrrhiza glabra* L.	Papilionaceae	Asthma	Root	One tea spoon full of root powder is taken orally
Shivani	*Gmelina arborea* Roxb.	Verbenaceae	Cuts and wounds	Leaves	Paste of crushed leaves is applied externally on wound part.
Kowri	*Grewia serrulata* DC.	Tiliaceae	Piles	Roots	One handful of root grounds in water and 1-2 tea spoon of juice are taken orally

Dasavala	*Hibiscus rosa-sinensis* L.	Malvaceae	Leucorrhoea	Flowers	Flowers macerated with seeds of cardamom and cumin is mixed with a cup of fresh cow's milk
Kadasiga	*Holarrhena pubescens* (Buch-Ham) Wall. ex. G.Don	Apocynaceae	Ring warm	Roots	Roots with bark of neem leaves made into paste and applied externally on infected area.
Tapasi	*Holoptelea integrifolia* (Roxb.) Planch.	Ulmaceae	herpes	Bark	Bark ground into paste and applied to affected area.
Adusoge	*Justicia adhatoda* L.	Acanthaceae	Cold and cough	Leaves	Pills are made out of crushed leaves and taken orally.
Chaduranga	*Lantana camara* L.	Verbenaceae	Wound	Leaves	Leaf juice applied externally with lime on wound, till cure
Tumbe	*Leucas aspera* (Wild.) Link	Laminaceae	Wound	Leaves	Use leaf paste
Muttidare muni	*Mimosa pudica* L.	Mimosaceae	Partial headache	Root	Root juice is poured (3-5 drops) in the ear lobes and nostrils.
Nugge	*Moringa oleifera* Lam.	Moringaceae	Blood pressure	Bark	Bark ground with lemon juice and mixed with a tea spoon of honey and cow' milk
Hoge soppu	*Nicotina tobacum* L.	Solanaceae	Scorpion sting	Leaves	Leaf juice of tobacco is taken orally with a cup of buttermilk.
Tulasi	*Ocimum tenuiflorum* L.	Lamiaceae	Eczema	Leaves	Leaf paste is mixed with turmeric is applied externally over wound part.
Hulisoppu	*Oxalis corniculata* L.	Oxalidaceae	Toothache	Leaves	Leaves ground into paste and applied on affected tooth
Chitramoola	*Plumbago zeylanica* L.	Plumbaginaceae	Eczema	Leaves	Leaves ash are applied externally on affected part with coconut oil.
Perale	*Psidium guajava* L.	Myrtaceae	Indigestion	Leaves	Tender leaves eaten daily morning orally.

Nerale	*Syzygium cumini* (L.) Skeels	Myrtaceae	Dysentery	Bark	One tea spoon of bark juice is taken orally.
Amruthaballi	*Tinospora cordifolia* (Willd.) Miers	Menisperm aceae	Boils	Leaves	Leaves ground with turmeric powder and pinch of salt to prepare a paste
Lakki	*Vitex negundo* L.	Verbenaceae	Fever	Leaves	Leaves boiled in water and the vapor is inhaled at least for 5min.
Parage	*Ziziphus oenoplia* (L.) Mil.	Rhamnaceae	Mouth ulcer	Root	Roots crushed in water and two tea spoon of paste taken orally

The people of age group 25 - 80 are giving traditional medicine in the study area and the majority of the people belong to 50 - 70 age group category. In the gender in volumes, male are giving more traditional medicine than female, but female are commonly use various home remedies for curing common fever, cold and other diseases. The traditional medicine system was more practice in interview, rural areas than the areas near to city or urban of the taluk. The Apocyanaceae family was the most commonly used family representing 43 % of all the medicinal plant species recorded by this study, followed by the Fabaceae at 19 %. The plant parts most frequently used were the roots (44 %), followed by the leaves (26 %), bark (15 %), the whole plant (11 %), and flowers and fruits (4 %). Most of the traditional healers obtained their extracts by boiling the medicinal plants. The most often recurring ailments treated by healers was stomach problems for both human and veterinary ailments, using 31 % of all medicinal plants reported in this study for preparing such treatments.

Table - 2: Plant species used to treat veterinary disorders

Vernacular name	Scientific name	Family	Growth farm	Part used	Diseases	Mode of Preparation
Gulaganji	*Abrus precatorius* (L.)	Papilionaceae	Tree	Leaves	Cough and Jaundice	Leaves paste used treat disease
Uttarani	*Achyranthus aspera* (L.)	Amaranthaceae	Herbs	Root	Maternity treatment	Root is grind in water
Baje	*Acorus calamus* L.	Acoraceae	Tree	Root	Heart diseases	Boiled in hot water with dry marry gold flower
Aadu muttada soppu	*Adhathoda zeylanica* Medik	Acanthaceae	Shrub	Leaves	Snake bite	Ground leaves are directly given.

Ankole	*Alangium salviifolium* (L.f) Wangerin	Cornaceae	Tree	Root	Fever	Ground root is given with the food.
Bilva patre	*Aegle marmelos* (L.) Correa	Rutaceae	Tree	Leaves	Gastritis joint pains	Leaves are ground with other ingredients and boiled in water and gives for 2 days
Maddale	*Alstonia scholaris* (L.) R. Br.	Apocynaceae	Tree	Leaves	Cold and Weakness	Leaves were crushed and used for disease
Ananas	*Ananas comosus* (L.) Merr.	Bromellaceae	Herb	Fruit	Constipation	Fruit juice is given to the animal
Uganiballi	*Argyreia elliptica* (Roth) Choisy	Convolvulaceae	Climber	Leaves	Ulcer in mouth and Pain in legs	Leaves were crushed and applied to pain part
Majjige gadde (Shatavari)	*Asparagus racemosus* wild.	Liliaceae	Herb	Roots and leaves	Galactagogue	Leaves and roots were crushed and give them to cattle
Manjepatre	*Artemisia nilagirica* (C.B. Clarke) Pamp.	Asteraceae	Herb	Leaves	Dry nose	Juice of leaves are put into the nose
Bevina mara	*Azadirachta indica* A. Juss.	Meliaceae	Tree	Leaves	Swelling knee	Leaves are ground and applied
Muttuga	*Butea monosperma* (Lam.) Tauber	Fabaceae	Tree	Leaves	Swellings	The plant part fried and mixed with other ingredients and boiled in water, the mixture is tied with cloth is affected area.
Gajagada soppu	*Ceasalpinia bonduc* (L.) Roxb.	Ceasalpinaceae	Tree	Leaves	Swellings	Ground leaves are applied to affected part.
Ekke	*Calatropis gigantia* (L.) Dryand	Asclepiadaceae	Shrub	Latex	Wounds in nose	Latex is mixed with coconut milk and given to the animal

Kavalu	*Careya arborea* Roxb.	Lecythidaceae	Tree	Seeds	Skin diseases	Seeds are mixed with garlic, pepper and butter milk given to the cattle.
Dalchinni	*Cinnamomum verum* J.S. Presi.	Laraceae	Tree	Bark	Infection	Dried part is powdered & applied on infected part.
Nela mavu	*Curcuma amada* Roxb.	Zingiberaceae	Herb	Root	Snake bite	ground rhizome is applied
Arishina	*Curcuma domastica* Valeton	Zingiberaceae	Herb	Rhizome	Bone fracture	Powdered of dried rhizome is mixed with egg and black gram tied with help of cloth.
Emmegedde	*Cyanotis tuberosa* (Roxb.) Schultes and Schutes f.	Commelinaceae	Herb	Root	Milk yield	Root is powdered and given with water
Vayubalaga	*Embelia ribes* N. Burm	Myrsinaceae	Herb	Leaves	Weakness	Leaves are ground and given to animal
Engu/Hingu	*Ferula assafoetida* L.	Apiaceae	Herb	Crystal line root	Cold and cough	Exudates mix with animal
Pundisoppu	*Hibiscus cannabinus* (L.)	Malvaceae	Tree	Leaves	Foot and mouth disease	Leaf paste mixed with buttermilk and given to cow
Tapasi	*Holoptelea integirifolia* (Roxb.) Planch	Ulmaceae		Bark and leaves	Cold and cough, weakness	Leaf mixed with garlic and given to animal
Dupanige	*Leea indica* (Burm.f.) Merr.	Vitaceae	Tree	Leaves	Dysentery and diarrhea	10 hand full leaf mixed with butter milk and give to animal
Thumbe	*Leucas aspera* (Wild.) Link	Lamiaceae	Herb	Leaves	Body ache and conjunctivitis.	Leaf juice poured to eye of animal
Kumkumada mara	*Mallotus philippensis* (Lam.) Muell. Arg.	Euphorbiaceae	Tree	Leaves	Snake bites	Mixed with leaves of drumstick & neem applied.

Muttidare muni	*Mimosa pudica* L.	Mimosaceae	Herb	Whole plants	During birth to young ones	Leaves are ground and applied
Nugge soppu	*Moringa oleifera* Lam.	Moringaceae	Tree	Leaves	Saliva in mouth	Leaves are ground with zinger, garlic, pepper and ajwana seeds mixed is given to the animal.
Nasagunni soppu	*Mucuna pruriens* (L.) DC.	Fabaceae		Leaves	Digestion problems	Leaves are crushed and given
Kamakasturi	*Ocimum tenui florum* L.	Lameaceae	Shrub	Leaves	Water in eyes	Juice of leaves are put into the eyes
Nelanelli	*Phyllanthus amarus* Schumach. and Thonn.	Phyllanthaceae	Herb	Whole plant	Bone fracture	Whole plant is ground with egg, turmeric powder, black gram. the mixture is bind to the affected part
Srigandha	*Santalum album* L.	Santalaceae	Tree	Stem	Horn diseases	Ground stem is mixed with other ingredients and applied to the horn
Elavarige	*Senna sophera* (L.) Roxb.	Caesalpiniaceae		Leaves	Wound and warms	Leaves paste is applied externally
Bili suli	*Securinega leucopyrus* (Wild.) Muell. Arg	Phyllanthaceae	Tree	Leaves	Worms on the wounds	Leaves are ground with tobacco leaves and applied to the affected part.
Baralu gida	*Sida acuta* N.Burm	Malvaceae	Shrub	Leaves	Infection	Leaves are ground and applied to the affected part
Chendu Hoovu	*Tagetes erecta* (L.)	Asteraceae	Shrub	Flower	Heart diseases	Dried flower is mixed with other ingredients and boiled in hot water

Maddarasa	*Tabernaemontana alternifolia* L.	Apocynaceae	Shrub	Bark	Snake bite	Bark paste is mixed with buttermilk and give to cow
Hunase	*Tamarindus indica* (L.)	Caesalpiniaceae	Tree	Leaves	Stomach pain	Juice of leaves is given
Tore matti	*Terminalia arjuna* (Roxb. Ex Dc) Wight and Arn.	Combretaceae	Tree	Bark	Ear ache andheart diseases	Bark is powder with honey and given to animal
Telakina soppu	*Tridax procumbens* L.	Asteraceae	Herb	Whole plants	Back pain and swelling on shoulders	Whole plant is ground and applied
Taare	*Terminalia bellirica* (Gaertn). Roxb.	Combretaceae	Tree	Bark	Foot and mouth diseases	Bark paste is given to cattle orally.
Uddina bele	*Vigna mungo* (L.) Hepper	Fabaceae	Shrub	Seeds	Bone fracture	Whole plant is ground with egg, turmeric powder, black gram the mixture is bind to the affected part
Shunti	*Zingiber officinale* Roscoe.	Zingiberaceae	Herb	Rhizome	Tympanitis	Rhizome crushed with *garlic* paste is given to animals

Certain plants used as medicine for treating diseases by local healers use *Achyranthes aspera* L. to cure gastric problems whereas the same plant is used for same purpose in the folk medicine of some villages in Shikaripura taluk of Shimoga district (Pandith *et al.*, 2009). *Calotropis gigantia* used to cure headache by local people. The same plant is used for the same purpose in Uttara kannada district (Chandrashekar *et al.*, 1995).

For snake bite local people use *Rauvulfia serpentina* and *Abrus precatorius* in combination. The Soligas use the *Rauvulfia serpentina* as a single source for the same. (Gopal *et al.* 1997) whereas Meitei community in Manipur use *Calotropis procera* for the same (Huidrom, 1997), *Rauwolfia serpentia* for the same by rural communities in selected villages of Shivamogga (Mahishi *et al.*, 2005). To treat Menorrhagia local

healers use *Oroxylum indicum* and *Tamarind indica* but Gowlis of Uttarkannada use only *Saraca indica* for the same ailment.

Cyclea peltata (Lam.) is used for intestinal worms. Whereas in villages of Bhadra wild life scantury *Citrus medica* is used for the same (Parinitha *et al.,* 2004). For cancer local healers use *Achyranthes aspera* and *Ludwigia perennis* in one combination and *Rauwolfia serpentina* and *Argyreia nervosa* in another combination. In Tiruvarur district Tamilnadu, *Dioscoria alata* tuber is used to cure cancer (Ajibade *et al.,* 2005) whereas *Clerodendrum serratum* was used to cure asthma by the Siddis of Uttarakannada (Bhandary *et al.,* 1995). For breast cancer *Plumbugo zeylanica* is used by rural communities in few villages of Shivamogga (Mahishi *et al.,* 2005). In veterinary treatment tribals use *Pothos scandens* and *Asparagus racemoses* as galactagogues. For bone fracture tribal's use *Curcuma domastica*.

For constipation local healers use *Ananas cosmosus* to treat cold in cattle's tribal's use *Piper longum* whereas the peoples of Kangra district used *Zinziber officinale* and *Trachyspermum ammi* for the same (Kanwar and Yadav, 2005; Prakasha and Krishnappa, 2006). The medicinal plant species used by the traditional healers are also used by many communities, tribes and folk medicine for the same purposes. There will be a need of phytochemical investigation for the medicinal plants used by this community to know very well the action of drugs on the particular ailment.

4. Conclusions

We have conducted documents of plants in selected villages of Shikaripura taluk. In the presence study it was found that people still utilize many species for their daily needs. Their livelihood is entirely dependent on their ecological surroundings and traditional healer use simple technology to sustainable their lifestyle, which seems totally conservative. The present study more focused on there is a profound and growing knowledge gap between younger and age old generations. People of more than 45 to 75 years age well know a lot about wild medicinal plant products when compare with younger generation. This study was conducted during the month of August 2018 to March 2019. A total 144 medicinal plant species listed in Shikaripura taluk, as we observed people in rural area gives a medicines for diseases like Itching, Scabies, Headache, Body pain, Bone fracture, Snake bites, Diabetes, Jaundice, skin diseases, malaria, tympanaties (ethno veterinary) etc.

During the survey, the peoples of the different age groups were interviewed for their traditional knowledge of phytomedicine for both human and veterinary. The information regarding the medicinal plants, preparation for medicine, dosages

etc. were collected by them. The plants were also collected for the herbarium from the interviewed person. During the visit it was noticed that some peoples were not ready to disclose the name of the plants due to their blind belief, if the identifying name of the plants is disclosed it may be loses its healing capacity. In such situations people were requested and detailed described and convinced them about the importance of the documentation of traditional knowledge for future use then only they agree to interact with us and explained what they know about local knowledge. The present documentation on ethnobotanical knowledge will help in wider dissemination of this knowledge and its long-term conservation. It also provides information on economy and social study of tribal and rural population.

5. References

1) Ajibade LT, Fatoba PO, Raheem UA, Odunnuga BA. Ethnomedicine and primary healthcare in Ilorin, Nigeria. Indian Journal of Traditional Knowledge 2005; 4(2):150-158.

2) Alexiades MN. Selected guidelines for Ethnobotanical research - A field manual. In Advances in Economic Botany, Vol.10. The New York Botanical Garden, Bronx, 1996.

3) Dhiman A, Vibhuti, Bhargava CAK. Medicinal importance of Papillionaceous plants of district Saharanpur, UP. Advanced plant Science 2008; 21(2): 597-601.

4) Bhandary MJ, Chandrashekar KR, Kaveriappa KM. Medical ethnobotany of the Siddis of Uttarakannada district, Karnataka, India. Journal of Ethnopharmacology 1995; 47(3): 149-158.

5) Bhatt DC, Mittaliya, Patel NK. Herbal remedies for renal calculli. Advances in Plant Science 2002; 15(1): 1-3.

6) Coton CM. Ethnobotany: principles and applications. John Willey and Sons Ltd., England, 1997.

7) Gopal GV, Jagadish Chandra KS. Ethnobotany of Soligas of Biligirirangana hills, Karnataka, India. Journal of Economic and Taxonomic Botany 2003; 8(2):12-16.

8) Jain SK. Dictionary of Indian folk medicine and ethnobotany. Deep publications, New Delhi, 1991.

9) Jouad H, Haloui.M, Rhiouani H, El Hilaiy J, Eddowes H. Ethnobotanical survey of medicinal plants used for the treatment of diabetes, cardiac and renal diseases in the north centre region of Morocco (Fez-Boulemane). Journal of Ethnopharmacology 2001; 77(2-3): 175-182.

10) Kandari LS, Gharai AK, Negi T, Phondani PC. Ethnobotanical knowledge of medicinal plants among tribal communities in Orissa, India. Forest Research 2012; 1: 104.

11) Kirtikar KP, Basu BT. Indian Medicinal Plants Vol-I, II, III and IV. International Book Distributors Dehradun, 1995.

12) Prakasha HM, Krishnappa M. People's knowledge on medicinal plants in Sringeri taluk, Karnataka. Indian Journal of Traditional Knowledge 2005; 5(3):353-357

13) Maheshwari JK, Kunkel G, Bhandari MM, Duke JA. Ethnobotany in India. Scientific Publishers, Jodhpur, 1993.

14) Martin GJ. Ethnobotany: A methods manual. WWF for Nature International, Chapman and Hall, London, UK, 1995.

15) Parinitha M, Harish GU, Vivek NC, Mahesh T, Shivanna MB. Ethnobotanical Wealth of Bhadra wildlife sanctuary in Karnataka. Indian Journal of Traditional Knowledge 2004; 3(1):37-50.

16) Parinitha M, Srinivasa BH, Shivanna MB. Medicinal plants wealth of local communities in some villages in Shimoga district of Karnaraka, India. Journal of Ethnopharmacology 2005; 98(3):307-312.

17) Prakasha HM, Krishnappa M. Herbal folk medicine used against cardiovascular and dental problems in N. R. Pura taluk, Karnataka. Advances in Plant Sciences 2006; 19(1): 203-208.

18) Kanwar P, Yadav D. Indigenous animal health care practices of Kangra district, Himachal Pradesh. Indian Journal of Traditional Knowledge 2005; 4(2):164-168.

19) Jha RK. Ethnomedicinal plants used against "Asthma" at Chhotanagpur, Jharkhand, India. Advanced Plant Science 2001; 14(I): 95-97.

20) Rajakumar N, Shivanna MB. Ethno-medicinal application of plants in the eastern region of Shimoga district, Karnataka, India. Journal of Ethnopharmacology 2009; 126(6): 64-73.

21) Rajiv Rai. Lesser known ethnomedicinal uses of tree species in Madhya Pradesh. Journal of Tropical Forestry 2009; 25(3): 65-74.

22) Ramaswamy SN, Rao MR, Govindappa DA. Flora of Shimoga District, Kamataka. Prasaranga, University of Mysore, Manasagangothri, Mysore, 2001.

23) Saldanha CJ, Nicolson DH. Flora of Hassan District, Karnataka, Vol. I. Oxford and IBH Publishing Co. Ltd., New Delhi, 1976.

24) Sanjay Kr Uniyal, Anjali Awasthi, Gopal Rawat. S. Traditional and ethnobotanical uses of plants in Bhagirathi valley (Western Himalaya). Indian Journal of Traditional Knowledge 2002; 1(1): 7-19.

25) Schultes RE. The role of the ethnobotanist in the search for new medicinal plants. Lyoydia 1962; 25: 257-262.

26) Shivanna MB, Rajakumar N. Traditional Medico-Botanical Knowledge of Local Communities in Hosanagara Taluk of Shimoga District in Karnataka, India. Journal of Herbs, Spices and Medicinal Plants 2011; 17(3): 291-317.

27) Singh Huidrom BK. Studies on medico Botany of Meitri community in Manipur State, India. Advances in Plant Sciences 1997; 10(1): 13-18.

28) Sinha RK. Ethnobotany- the renaissance of traditional herbal medicine. Ina Shree Publishers, Jaipur, India, 1996.

29) Suresha S, Jayashankar M, Vinu AK. Medicinal Plants Diversity in Muthathi Wild Life Sanctuary, Karnataka, India. Indian Journal of Pharmaceutical and Biological Research 2018; 6(3):13-22.

30) Yoganarsimhan SN, Subramanyam K, Razi BA. Flora of Chikmagalur district, Karnataka, India. International Book Distributors, Dehradun, 1981.

Cite this chapter as:

Vinayaka KS, Arpitha AG, Kekuda PTR. Ethnobotanical survey of Shikaripura Taluk, Shivamogga District, Karnataka, India. In: Kekuda PTR, Vinayaka KS, Raghavendra HL (Editors), Nature and Medicine: Traditional uses, chemistry and bioprospecting of natural products. JPS Scientific Publications, Tamil Nadu, India, 2020, Pp 11 - 29.

Nature and Medicine: Traditional Uses, Chemistry and Bioprocessing of Natural Products
ISBN: 978-81-947154-3-6
First Edition; 2020
Chapter – 3, Page: 30 - 37

3

DOCUMENTATION OF VEDIC PLANTS OF DAKSHINA KANNADA, KARNATAKA

Manohara Acharya

Department of Botany, Canara College, Mangaluru – 575 003, Dakshina Kannada, Karnataka, India

*Corresponding author: acharya.manohara@gmail.com

Abstract

Dakshina Kannada District is one of the integral parts of Parashurama srushti. It is well known for temples, seashores, and mountains. People of this area are performing religious rituals such as Pooja, Homa, Hawana, and Yaga, etc. during festivals, temple renovations (Pratishta and Brahmakalashotsava), marriage, housewarming ceremonies, upanayana, death rituals, etc since the Vedic period. Several sacred plants are used in Vedic rituals and are called as Vedic plants; no rituals will take place without these plants. In an attempt to preserve the fundamental knowledge of such plants, the present study was undertaken and some of the Vedic plants are documented along with their botanical name, local name, family, part used for rituals etc.

Key words: Vedic Plants, Vedic Period and Temple renovations.

1. Introduction

The oldest scripture of Indian Vedas were composed in 2500Bc to 600 BC. It is said that the study of classification and naming of plants in India is even older than those of Greeks and Romans. There are three groups of plants such as tree (Vriksha), herbs (Osadhi) and creepers (Virudh) have been recognized in the Rigvedic period.

The shape and Morphology of plants are also described in the Atharvaveda. The four groups of medicinal plants are described in the Yajurveda (Indian scriptures, 2017 and Flora of Indian epic 2017).

Sacred plants worshiping was also present during the Vedic period (Bhatla *et al.*, 1984). These are considered as the incarnations or symbols of God or deities and therefore this worship became more common because they played a very important in the myth and customs of India, without these plants and their products, religious and cultural rituals are not completed (Pandey and Pandey, 2016).

The plants were deeply rooted in the day to day life of human being. The cultures, customs, ethos, folk tales, folk songs, food and medicinal practices are associated and influenced by the plants (Badoni and Badoni, 2001). All people use one or several plants in the religious festivals and ceremonies (Bajpai *et al.*, 2016). The plants have vital role in human welfare and are continued to be valued industrial, economic, commercial and medicinal resources and some subcontinent even today in common uses much of which is steadily being eroded. Even in our traditional worship practices shown that there was a symbiotic relation in between human being and nature. Therefore, indigenous communities in India and elsewhere in the world, lived in harmony with nature and conserved its valuable Biodiversity (Dastur, 1951; Mitra, 1922; Schulted, 1960).

India has a deep rooted tradition of nature worship, which provides a base for conservation from the grassroots (Gadgil, 1987; Gadgil, 2000). The Hindu scripture tells us the importance of plants and a wide range of plants has divine qualities and used in many religious activities and rituals from marriage, baptism to healthcare systems (Robinson and Cush, 1997). In this article, documented the Vedic plants that were used in Vedic Vana's and Hawanas's across Dakshina Kannada district.

2. Methodology

2.1. Study area

Dakshina Kannada district (South Canara) is a district of Karnataka state; it is bordered by Udupi district to the north, Chikamagaluru district to the northeast, Hassan district to the east, Kodagu to the southeast and Kasaragod district of Kerala to the south i.e. 12.8438° N, 75.2479° E (Figure - 1). The District with its headquarters in the port city of Mangalore. It covers an area nestled in between the lush green Western Ghats to its east and Arabian sea to its west. It comprises seven taluks such as Mangalore, Putturu, Sillia, Bantwala, Belthangady, Kadaba and Moodbidri.

The major rivers join Arabian Sea, such as Netravathi, Kumaradhara, Gurupura, Shambavi, Nandini and Pavaswini. The Netravathi and Kumaradhara meet at Uppinangadi during Monsoon. This event is called "Sangam" which in Sanskrit means confluence. An 'Estuary' formed near Mangalore by the union of River Netravathi and the Gurupura which merge into the Arabian Sea. The abundant rain fall received by Dakshina Kannada during Monsoon. The average annual rain fall is 4,030 mm (159 inch). The rainfall varies from 3,774.1 mm (149 inch) to the Mangalore coast 4,530 mm (178 inch) at Moodubidire and 4,329 mm (170 inch) at Puttur near the Western Ghats. The average humidity is 75 % and peaks in July at 89 %.

The people living in Dakshina Kannada were known as 'Tuluvas' beacuase they spoke Tulu language. The different communities living together in Tulunadu such as Billava, Mogaveera, Bunt, Kulala, Tulu gowda and Devadiga are the largest ethnic group in the District. The people like Konkani, Brahmins, Holeyas, the hill tribes (Koragas), Muslims, Mangalorean catholics and arebhashe gowdas were added to the Tuluva population. The Brahmins consist of Shivalli, Saraswath, Vishwakarma, Havyakas, Chitpavan, Daivajna and Kota subsections also resides in Tulinadu. Tulu, Konkani, Kannada, Beary Bhashe, Malayalam, Arebhashe, Deccani, Urdu and Havyaka are the prominent languages spoken by people of Dakshina Kannada (Dakshina Kannada, 2020).

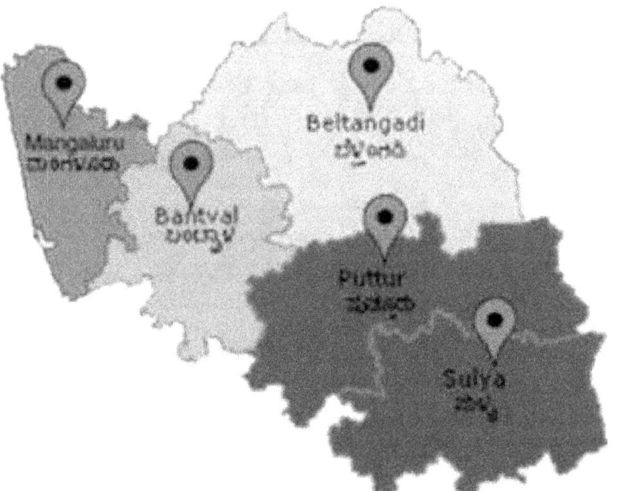

Figure - 1: Map of Dakshina Kannada

2.2. Documentation

Vedic vana's or Vedic plants are predominantly found in a majority of the temples and Botanical gardens of schools and colleges of Dakshina Kannada District. Vedic rituals are frequently performed in every Hindu house and temple of Dakshina Kannada. The documentation of Vedic plants were done by visiting the vana's of temples, botanical garden, referring Vedic literature, and by interviewing purohits (Priests) and botanists by standard questionnaire (Martin,1995).

3. Results and Conclusion

Dakshina Kannada is rich in Vedic Rituals as well as Plant diversity. There are different types of Vedic vanas such as Navagraha Vana (Nava - Nine, Graha - Planets, Vana – Garden), Rashivana (In Astrology there are 12 Zodiac signs. These 12 trees represent each one of them), Nakshatra Vana (Nakshatra - Stars [27], Vana– Garden), Santhana Vana (Santana-Children, Vanam-Garden, Childless women go around these trees to get conceived), Panchavati Vana (Pancha - Five, Vati – Trees: Rama along with Sita and Lakshmana spent 14 years of Vanavasa), Nandana Vana (Lord Indra's garden in the heaven is called Nandanavanam), Brinda Vana (Brinda - Group, Vanam – Garden - Different types of *Ocimum* species), Saptharishi Vana (The Saptarishi are the seven rishis in ancient India) and Shiva panchayathana vana which were built-in majority of the temples and botanical gardens of Schools and Colleges (Vedic Vanas, 2015).

The main aim of the Vedic Vanas is conserving Vedic plants, literate the youths regarding nature, health care, and spiritual significance of the Vedic plants. Veda and Vedic rituals taught us to use medicinal plants in different Vedic rituals such as Festivals, Homa, Hawana, Yaga, Pratista brahmakaloshotsava, Marriage, Upanayana, House warming ceremony and even in Death rituals also. But we are knowingly or unknowingly following all these Vedic rituals meanwhile using these medicinal plants also in our lives. The ultimate goal of Veda, Vedic Vana, and Vedic rituals are keeping Nature and human being healthy and spiritually strong. It has also taught us to live in nature without damaging nature by a sustainable method.

In this work, 50 Vedic plants belonging to 23 families and 41 genera are recorded of which 9 species belong to Leguminosae, 7 species to Lamiaceae and 6 species to Moraceae. Rest of the species recorded belongs to other families. As Veda and Vedic rituals have a lot of information regarding nature, science, health, wealth, spirituality and patriotism. Following Veda and Vedic rituals with knowledge will be helpful for mankind.

Table 1: Vedic plants documented in Dakshina Kannada

Plants Name	Local Name (Kan/San)	Vedic rituals
Acacia catechu (L.f.) Willd.	Kaachu/Khadira	Nakshatra Vana,Navagraha Vna, Navagraha Homa, Rashivana, Shiva panchayatana Vana
Achyranthes aspera L.	Uttarani	Navagraha Vana, Navagraha Homa, Saptarishi
Adansonia digitata L.	Anehunase/Kalpavriksh	Nandana vana
Aegle marmelos (L.) Corrêa	Bilva/Bilva	Nakshatra Vana, Shiva panchayatanavana, Panchavati, Saptarissi vana
Alstonia scholaris (L.) R. Br.	Haale mara/Saptaparni	Rashivana
Aquilaria agallocha Roxb.	Agaru/Agaru	Nakshatra Vana
Artocarpus heterophyllus Lam.	Halsu/Panasa	Nakshatra Vana, Rashivana
Azadirachta indica A.Juss.	Kahibevu/Nimbaka	Nakshatra Vana, Santhana vana, Nandana vana
Bambusa bambos (L.) Voss	Bidiru/vamsh	Nakshatra Vana
Bauhinia purpurea L.	Kanchivala/ Devakanchan	Nandana vana
Bombax ceiba L.	Kempu booruga / Shalmali	Nakshatra Vana
Butea monosperma (Lam.) Taub.	Muttuga/Palasha	Nakshatra Vana, Navagraha Vana Navagraha Homa, Rashivana
Calophyllum inophyllum L.	Honne /Punnaga	Nakshatra Vana
Calotropis procera (Aiton) Dryand.	Ekka/Arka	Nakshatra Vana, Navagraha Homa, Shivapanchayatana vana
Canarium strictum Roxb.	Rala doopa/Raal	Nakshatra Vana
Clitoria ternatea L.	Shanka Pushpa	Shiva panchayata vana
Cynodon dactylon (L.) Pers.	Garike/Doorva	Navagraha Vana, Navagraha homa, Ganahoma, Shiva panchayatana vana, Saptharishi vana
Dalbergia sissoo DC.	Shimshape/Aguru	Radhivana
Datura metel L.	Unmatta gida	Saptarishi vana
Ficus benghalensis L.	Aala /vatavruksha	Nakshatra Vana, Nandanavana
Ficus benghalensis L.	Aala/ Vatavruksha	Rashivana, Panchavati
Ficus infectoria Willd.	Basari mara/Plaksha	Nakshatra Vana
Ficus racemosa L.	Atti/Audumbara	Nakshatra Vana, Navagraha Vana, Navagraha Homa, Panchavati
Ficus religiosa L.	Arali/Ashwatha	Nakshatra Vana, Rashivana, Shiva panchayathanavana, Santhana vana, Panchavati, Nandana vana
Imperata ylindrical (L.) Raeusch.	Dharbe/Kusha	Navagraha Vana, All Homa

Leucas aspera (Willd.) Link	Tumbe	Shiva panchayata vana
Limonia acidissima L.	Bela /Kapitha	Nakshatra Vana
Madhuca longifolia var. latifolia (Roxb.) A.Chev.	Ippe/Madhuka	Nakshatra Vana
Mangifera indica L.	Maavu/aamru	Nakshatra Vana, Rashivana, Nandana vana
Mimusops elengi L.	Renje/Bakula	Nakshatra Vana, Rashivana
Neolamarckia cadamba (Roxb.) Bosser	Apatti/Kadamba	Nakshatra Vana,Nadana vana
Nerium oleander L.	Kanagilu	Shiva panchayata vana
Ocimum × africanum Lour.	Nimbe tulasi	Vrinda vana
Ocimum americanum L.	Nayi tulasi	Vrinda vana
Ocimum basilicum L.	Kama kasturi	Vrinda vana
Ocimum gratissimum L.	Lavanga Tulasi	Vrinda vana
Ocimum kilimandscharicum Gürke	Karpura tulasi	Vrinda vana
Ocimum tenuiflorum L.	Tulasi, Rma tulasi/ Krishna tulasi	Shiva panchayata vana, Vrinda vana, Saptarishi vana
Phyllanthus emblica L.	Bettada Nelli/Dhatri	Nakshatra Vana, Panchavati
Pinus palustris Mill.	Soochprnada mara	Nandana Vana
Prosopis cineraria (L.) Druce	Banni/Shami	Nakshatra Vana, Navagra homa, Rashivana, Saptarishi vana
Pterocarpus santalinus L.f.	Rakatachandana	Rashivana
Santalum album L.	Shrregandha, Chandana	Nandana vana
Saraca asoca (Roxb.) Willd.	Ashoka/sita Ashoka	Nakshatra Vana, Panchayatana vana, Ashoka vana
Sesbania grandiflora (L.) Pers.	Agase	Saptarishi vana
Spondias pinnata (L. f.) Kurz	Ambate/Ambaste	Nakshatra Vana
Stereospermum chelonoides (L.f.) DC.	Paadri/Patala	Rashivana
Strychnos nux-vomica L.	Kasrakka/Karaskara	Nakshatra Vana
Syzygium cumini (L.) Skeels	Nerale/Jamboo	Nakshatra Vana,Nandana vana
Terminalia arjuna (Roxb. Ex DC.) Wight & Arn.	Bilimatti/Arjuna	Nakshatra Vana,Pratiste

5. References

1) Badoni A and Badoni K. 2001. Ethnobotanical heritage in Garhwal Himalaya: Nature, Culture and Society, Kandari OP and Gusain OP, (Editors). Transmedia, Srinagar Garhwal.

2) Bajpai O, Pandey J, Chaudhary LB. Ethnomedicinal uses of tree species by Tharu tribes in the Himalayan Terai region of India. Research Journal of Medicinal Plant 2016; 10(1): 19-41.

3) Bhatla N, Mukherjee T, Singh G. Plants: Traditional worshipping. Indian Journal of History of Science 1984; 19(1): 37-42.

4) Dastur JF. Useful Plants of India and Pakistan. D.B. Taraporewala Sons & Co. Ltd. Bombay, India, 1951.

5) Gadgil M. Diversity: cultural and ecological, Trends in Ecology and Evolution 1987; 2(12): 369-373.

6) Gadgil M. 2000. Grass roots conservation practices: Revitalizing the traditions, In: Communities and conservation - Natural resources management in South and Central Asia. Kothari A, Pathak N, Anuradha RV, Taneja B (Editors), Sage Publication, New Delhi. Pp 220-237.

7) Mitra SC. On the Cultivation of the tree-goddess in Eastern Bengal. Man in India 1922; 5: 115-131.

8) Martin GJ. Ethnobotany: A method manual. Chapman and Hall, London, 1995.

9) Pandey D, Pandey VC. Sacred plants from ancient to modern era: Traditional worshipping towards plants conservation. Tropical Plant Research 2016; 3(1):136-141.

10) Schulted RE. Tapping our heritage of ethno-botanical lore. Economic Botany 1960; 14: 257-262.

Cite this chapter as:

Manohara Acharya. Documentation of Vedic plants of Dakshina Kannada, Karnataka. In: Kekuda PTR, Vinayaka KS, Raghavendra HL (Editors), Nature and Medicine: Traditional uses, Chemistry and Bioprospecting of Natural Products. JPS Scientific Publications, Tamil Nadu, India, 2020, Pp 30 - 37.

Nature and Medicine: Traditional Uses, Chemistry and Bioprocessing of Natural Products
ISBN: 978-81-947154-3-6
First Edition; 2020
Chapter – 4, Page: 38 - 50

4

AN INCLUSIVE REVIEW ON ETHNOBOTANICAL USES OF *Anogeissus latifolia* (Combretaceae) IN INDIA

Mahalakshmi S. N[1] and Prashith Kekuda T. R[2*]

[1]Department of Zoology, S.R.N.M.N College of Applied Sciences, NES Campus, Balraj Urs Road, Shivamogga – 577 201, Karnataka, India
[2]Department of Microbiology, S.R.N.M.N College of Applied Sciences, NES Campus, Balraj Urs road, Shivamogga – 577 201, Karnataka, India
*Corresponding author: p.kekuda@gmail.com

Abstract

Anogeissus latifolia (Roxb. ex DC.) Wall. ex Bedd. belonging to the family Combretaceae is an important tree species having several ethnobotanical applications. The plant is used traditionally as medicine to treat various human ailments and conditions such as vomiting, whooping cough, cold, diarrhea, dysentery, snake and scorpion bite, fever, skin diseases, diabetes, anemia, piles, fistula, stomach ache, sexual debility, anemia, and urinary discharge. The gum (ghatti gum) extracted from the plant is also having several therapeutic applications. Different parts such as seeds and stem bark of A. latifolia find ethnoveterinary applications and are used to treat snake bite, insect bite, fever and other veterinary ailments. Besides, the plant is also used as fodder and in making things such as pole, door, and cart axle. This multifold ethnobotanical applications of A. latifolia strongly highlights the need for conservation of this plant species and cultivation of the plant

for its potential uses.

Key words: *Anogeissus latifolia*, Ethnobotanical uses, Ethnomedicinal and Ethnoveterinary

1. Introduction

Humans depend on plants for meeting various needs such as food, cloth, construction tools and medicine. Since time immemorial, plants have been exploited by people for treating various kinds of human and veterinary ailments. Either singly or in polyherbal formulations, many plant species are used in various indigenous systems of medicines. Few examples for the most popular indigenous systems of medicine that utilize plants are Ayurveda, Unani, Siddha, Homeopathy and Traditional Chinese medicine. Exploitation of medicinal plants is often a way for generating income by some rural communities. Phytochemicals such as polyphenols, terpenes and alkaloids are known to exert several health benefits and are responsible for pharmacological properties of the plants. The chemical nature of these phytochemicals provides leads for developing novel therapeutic agents. Compounds such as morphine, vincristine, vinblastine, artemisinin, quinine and digoxin are from plant origin. Plant based medicines are affordable, available locally and are generally free from side effects (Jain *et al.*, 2005; Vaidya and Devasagayam, 2007; Ravishankar and Shukla, 2007; Kala, 2009; Galav *et al.*, 2013; Sen and Chakraborty, 2016; Khonde *et al.*, 2017).

Anogeissus latifolia (Roxb. ex DC.) Wall. ex Bedd.

A. latifolia belongs to the family Combretaceae. It is a tree species (reaching 20 to 35 m in length) found distributed in semi-evergreen and deciduous forests of different states of India. It is one of the tree species yielding gum with medicinal values. It is commonly known as Axle wood tree or Ghatti tree. The plant is valuable as a fodder, fuel, timber and medicinal plant. It is one of the secondary food plants for tropical tasar silkworm. The leaves as well as the bark of the tree are used for tanning. Different parts viz. bark, gum and root of *A. latifolia* find medicinal importance in various indigenous systems of medicine. *A. latifolia* is one of the ingredients in several Ayurvedic formulations. The stem bark of *A. latifolia* is one of the ingredients of an Ayurvedic formulation Ayaskrti (Orwa et al., 2009; Katekhaye and Bhutani, 2011; Sivaraj *et al.*, 2017; Yadav *et al.*, 2017; Dinesh, 2018). In Bangladesh, the plant is traditionally used in the treatment of snake bite (Hasan *et al.*, 2016). The gum (designated as ghatti gum) obtained from the plant has several applications including medicinal values. The gum is used in calico printing. The gum is also used as stabilizer, emulsifier and thickener in food and pharmaceuticals. It is

also used as drilling mud conditioner in petroleum industry (Kala, 2016; Chouhan and Sudip, 2017). In this review, we provide comprehensive detail on various ethnobotanical uses of *A. latifolia* in India.

Classification

Kingdom	:	Plantae
Subkingdom	:	Tracheobionta
Superdivision	:	Spermatophyta
Division	:	Magnoliophyta
Class	:	Magnoliopsida
Subclass	:	Rosidae
Order	:	Myrtales
Family	:	Combretaceae
Genus	:	*Anogeissus* (DC.) Wall.
Species	:	*Anogeissus latifolia* (Roxb. ex DC.) Wall. ex Beddome

2. Ethnomedicinal applications of *A. latifolia*

Literature survey revealed a number of medicinal uses of different parts of *A. latifolia* for the treatment of several human ailments. In Balaghat district, Madhya Pradesh, India, the poultice of stem bark is applied externally to treat hernia (Jain *et al.*, 2011). The Garasia tribe of Sirohi district, Rajasthan uses the fresh bark to cure cough and the gum after delivery (Meena and Yadav, 2011). The plant (root, leaf and fruit) finds ethnomedicinal uses as antiseptic and is used to treat wounds, tumor and cancer, rheumatism and burning sensation by tribal community in Dindori district, Madhya Pradesh, India (Marko and Sandya, 2020). The tribal communities in Adilabad district, Andhra Pradesh use stem bark of *A. latifolia* to relieve stomachache (Murthy, 2012). In the Aravalli ranges in North Gujarat, the stem bark is used to cure cough (Punjani and Kumar, 2002). The tribal communities of Saputara Hill, Dang district, Gujarat use the gum with water in early morning for lactation (Patel and Varshney, 2017). Laddu and few other sweets prepared using several plant species including *A. latifolia* is consumed in Udaipur city, Rajasthan to increase endurance against cold (Jain, 2020). In Khammam district, Andhra Pradesh, India, the stem bark is chewed and the sap is swallowed to relieve persistent cough (Reddy *et al.*, 2008).

In Vizianagaram district, Andhra Pradesh, the wood ash is use to wash hairs to relieve from dandruff (Rao *et al.*, 2014). The gum of *A. latifolia* is used traditionally for the treatment of menorrhea in Eastern Ghats, Andhra Pradesh (Ratnam *et al.*, 2019). In Mysore and Coorg districts, Karnataka, the bark is used to check vomiting

sensation (Kshirsagar and Singh, 2001). In Chitrakoot, Madhya Pradesh, the stem bark is used to treat snake bite and diarrhea (Misra, 2015). In Mandal tehsil, Bhilwara, Rajasthan, the gum is used to cure sexual debility (Singh and Meena, 2018). The powder prepared from the dried fruits is used to relieve stomach ache in Thane district, Maharashtra (Natarajan and Paulsen, 2000). In Terai region, Uttar Pradesh, the bark is given in anemia and urinary diseases (Bajpai *et al.*, 2016). The gum is used in skin diseases and sciatic pain in Eastern ghats of Vizianagaram district, Andhra Pradesh, India (Parijatham *et al.*, 2016). In Adilabad district of Telangana state, the stem bark is used for treatment of asthma and scorpion bite (Ramakrishna *et al.*, 2015). Different parts of the plant are useful in skin diseases, diarrhea and dysentery in Mandaragiri, Angul forest division, Odisha, India (Pradhan *et al.*, 2014). The tribal community in Guna district, Madhya Pradesh use different parts such as fruit, root and leaves of the plant as antiseptic and to treat wound, tumor and cancer, rheumatism and burning sensation (Samar *et al.*, 2015). More information on ethnomedicinal importance of *A. latifolia* is provided in Table 1.

Table - 1: Medicinal uses of A. latifolia

Area	Part used	Uses	Reference
Toranmal plateau of Maharashtra, India	Bark	Vomiting	Sharma and Mujumdar (2003)
Maharashtra, India	Bark	To ease delivery	Kamble *et al.* (2010)
Nasik district, Maharashtra, India	Stem bark	Whooping cough	Patil and Patil (2005)
Northwest Maharashtra, India	Bark	Dysentery	Kamble *et al.* (2008)
Dhule and Jalgaon districts, Maharashtra, India	Bark	Vomiting	Jain *et al.* (2010a)
Dang's district, South Gujarat, India	Bark	Liver problems	Kumar (2015)
Bilaspur, Hamirpur and Una districts, Himachal Pradesh, India	Bark, flowers, fruits, roots, stems	Wound, diarrhoea, Diabetes	Bhardwaj and Seth (2017)
Alirajpur district, Madhya Pradesh, India	Gum	To increase strengh after delivery	Chouhan and Sudip (2017)
Rewa district, Madhya Pradesh, India	Bark	Diarrhoea	Shukla *et al.* (2010)
Southern Rajastan, India	Gum	Used after delivery in the form of laddu	Meena and Yadav (2010)
Betul district, Madhya Pradesh, India	Stem bark	Cough and cold	Jain *et al.* (2010b)
Banda district, Uttar Pradesh, India	Stem bark	Snake bite and diarrhoea	Mishra (2015a)
Tikamgarh district, Madhya Pradesh, India	Root	Fever	Ahirwar *et al.* (2017)

Dindigul district, Tamil Nadu, India	Gum	Skin diseases	Sundaram and Suresh (2019)
Jharkhand, India	Bark	Skin diseases	Kumar and Abbas (2012)
Surguja district, Chhttishgarh, India	Bark	Diabetes	Shrivastava and Kanungo (2013)
Maharashtra, India	Stem bark	Urinary trouble	Kamble *et al.* (2014)
Dindori district, Madhya Pradesh, India	Fried gum	Spermatorrhoea	Singh and Ahirwar (2018)
Dang district, Gujarat, India	Bark	Anemia, urinary discharge, piles and snake bite	Patel and Varshney (2017)
Prakasam district, Andhra Pradesh, India	Stem bark	Cough, dysentery	Reddy *et al.* (2012)
Kerala, India	Bark	Diarrhoea	Thomas *et al.* (2013)
Uttar Pradesh, India	Bark, gum	Hair tonic	Shankar *et al.* (2017)
Maharashtra, India	Gum	Lactation	Jagtap *et al.* (2009)
Nanded district, Maharashtra, India	Seed	Respiratory disorders	Reddy (2017)
Nanded district, Maharashtra, India	Whole plant	Piles and fistula	Reddy and Kashinath (2016)
Rewa and Sidhi District of Madhya Pradesh, India	Bark	Vomiting	Bharti *et al.* (2013)
Parthapgah district, Rajasthan, India	Bark	Snake bite	Kumar and Sharma (2018)
Nasik and Dhule districts, Maharashtra, India	Bark	Snake bite	Kuvar and Shinde (2019)
Nimar region, Madhya Pradesh, India	Bark	Cough	Jeetendra and Jeetendra (2015)
South east Rajasthan, India	Leaf	Wound	Arora and Jain (2018)
Uttar Pradesh, India	Bark	Astringent	Shankar *et al.* (2016)
Central India	Whole plant	Snake bite	Kadel and Jain (2008)
Godavari district, Andhra Pradesh, India	-	Scorpion sting, snake bite	Divya *et al.* (2015)
Similipal biosphere reserve, Odisha, India	Bark	Diarrhoea	Panda *et al.* (2017)

3. Ethnoveterinary uses of *A. latifolia*

Several indigenous plant species have been extensively used to treat veterinary ailments by several tribal communities across the world (Galav *et al.*, 2013; Saganuwan *et al.*, 2013; Meena, 2014). It is shown from several studies that *A. latifolia* possess medicinal importance with respect to treatment of diseases of animals and livestock. The gum obtained from the plant is used to treat wounds (Nair *et al.*, 2017). The decoction prepared from the bark of *A. latifolia* is used to treat fever in livestock in Rajasthan, India (Galav *et al.*, 2013). The tribal communities in eastern Ghats of Andhra Pradesh, India use the plant to treat ephemeral fever (Reddy *et al.*, 2006). In the north coastal districts of Andhra Pradesh, India, the plant is used to treat ephemeral fever (Lakshminarayana and Rao, 2013). More information on ethnoveterinary significance of *A. latifolia* is presented in Table - 2.

Chapter - 4

Table - 2: Ethnoveterinary applications of A. latifolia

Area	Part used	Uses	Reference
Bhandara district (M.S.) India	Stem bark	Dysentery	Gadpayale *et al.* (2011)
Rayala seema region, Andhra Pradesh, India	Seed	Insect and snake bite	Reddy *et al.* (2016)
Rayala seema region, Andhra Pradesh, India	Stem bark	Horne cancer, fever, cataplasm, skin disease, tymphany	Reddy *et al.* (2016)
Ganjam district, Odisha, India	Bark	Painful delivery	Mishra (2015b)
Pathardi tahasil, Ahmednagar district (M.S.) India	Stem bark	Dysentery	Ashok *et al.* (2012)
Sariska region, Rajasthan, India	Bark	Ephemeral fever	Upadhyay *et al.* (2011)

4. Other uses of *A. latifolia*

Besides medicinal uses, *A. latifolia* is also used for other purposes such as construction, fodder, fibre, fuel and ritualistic purposes. *A. latifolia* is utilized as fodder and fibre in foot hills of Garhwal Himalaya (Kumar and Bhatt, 2006). In Rajsamand district of Rajasthan, India, *A. latifolia* is used to make rehat (a traditional irrigation system), axle of the wheel and pitcher stands (Choudhary *et al.*, 2008). Table 3 presents information on ethnobotanical uses of *A. latifolia* other than medicinal uses.

Table - 3: Uses of A. latifolia other than medicinal uses

Area	Part used	Uses	References
Dangs district, Gujarat, India	Wood, bark	Charcoal, cart axle, tannin	Kumar *et al.* (2007)
Boudh district, Odisha, India	Stem wood	Charcoal, paper pulp industry	Sahu *et al.* (2013)
Kalakad Mundan-thurai tiger reserve, Southern India	Wood	Construction of hut	Ayyanar and Ignacimuthu (2010)
Sitamata Wildlife Sanctuary of Rajasthan, India	Tender branches, stem	Framework of windows, roof and doors	Meena *et al.* (2013)
Wayanad Wildlife Sanctuary, Kerala, India	Wood	Fire wood	Narayanan *et al.* (2011)
Wayanad Wildlife Sanctuary, Kerala, India	Resin from stem	Ritualistic purposes	Narayanan *et al.* (2011)
Mysore district, Karnataka	Stem	Fuel wood	Nandini and Shiddamallayya (2015)
Sunabeda Wildlife Sanctuary, Orissa, India	Stem	Fire wood, house construction	Sabar (2014)

5. Conclusions

An extensive literature survey that we carried out indicated potential benefits of different parts especially bark of *A. latifolia* in terms of its marked medicinal and other properties. The plant is extensively used in the country for treating several human and veterinary ailments. Moreover, the stem or wood of the plant is used in several construction activities. It is important for us to conserve this plant species as the plant is reported to possess multiple beneficial uses of humans.

5. References

1) Ahirwar RP, Tripathi J, Singh R. Ethnomedicinal study of plants used by Tribal person for fever diseases in Tikamgarh district M.P. International Journal of Botany Studies 2017; 2(3): 64-67.

2) Arora A, Jain S. Ethnomedicinal documentation of antimicrobial plants from south east Rajasthan, India. The Journal of Phytopharmacology 2018; 7(2): 203-206.

3) Ashok SP, Sonawane BN, Reddy DPG. Traditional ethno-veterinary practices in Karanji Ghat areas of Pathardi tahasil in Ahmednagar district (M.S.) India. International Journal of Plant, Animal and Environmental Sciences 2012; 2(1): 64-69.

4) Bajpai O, Pandey J, Chaudhary LB. Ethnomedicinal Uses of Tree Species by Tharu Tribes in the Himalayan Terai Region of India. Research Journal of Medicinal Plant 2016; 10(1): 19-41.

5) Bhardwaj J, Seth MK. Medicinal plant resources of Bilaspur, Hamirpur and Una districts of Himachal Pradesh: An ethnobotanical enumeration. Journal of Medicinal Plants Studies 2017; 5(5): 99-110.

6) Bharti RP, Shrivastava A, Choudhary JR, Tiwari A, Soni NK. Ethno Medicinal Plants used by Tribal Communities in Vindhya region of Rewa and Sidhi District of Madhya Pradesh, India. IOSR Journal of Pharmacy and Biological Sciences 2013; 8(6): 23-28.

7) Choudhary BL, Katewa SS, Galav PK. Plants in material culture of tribals and rural communities of Rajsamand district of Rajasthan. Indian Journal of Traditional Knowledge 2008; 7(1): 11-22.

8) Chouhan DS, Sudip R. Ethnomedicinal plants and plant parts sold in the local market by herbal healers in Alirajpur district, Madhya Pradesh. Indian Journal of Plant Sciences 2017; 6(1): 27-31.

9) Dinesh B. Pollen biology and morphology of *Anogeissus latifolia*, (Roxb. ex DC) Wall. ex Bedd. (Combretaceae). International Journal of Botany Studies 2018; 3(2): 121-123.

10) Divya K, Roja MN, Padal SB. Ethno-medicinal plants used in east Godavari district, Andhra Pradesh, India. International Journal of Pharmacological Research 2015; 5(11): 293-300.

11) Gadpayale JV, Khobragade DP, Chaturvedi AA. Traditional Ethno-Veterinary practices in Bhandara district (M.S.) India. International Journal of Sciences & Applied Research 2014; 1(2): 91-99.

12) Galav P, Jain A, Katewa SS. Ethnoveterinary medicines used by tribals of Tadgarh-Raoli wildlife sanctuary, Rajasthan, India. Indian Journal of Traditional Knowledge 2013; 12(1): 56-61.

13) Galav P, Jain A, Katewa SS. Traditional veterinary medicines used by livestock owners of Rajasthan, India. Indian Journal of Traditional Knowledge 2013; 12(1): 47-55.

14) Hasan MN, Azam NK, Ahmed MN, Hirashima A. A randomized ethnomedicinal survey of snakebite treatment in southwestern parts of Bangladesh. Journal of Traditional and Complementary Medicine 2015; 6(4): 337-342.

15) Jagtap SD, Deokule SS, Pawar PK, Harsulkar AM. Traditional Ethnomedicinal Knowledge Confined to the Pawra Tribe of Satpura Hills, Maharashtra, India. Ethnobotanical Leaflets 2009; 13: 98-115.

16) Jain A, Katewa SS, Galav PK. Some phytotherapeutic claims by tribals of Southern Rajasthan. Indian Journal of Traditional Knowledge 2005; 4(3): 291-297.

17) Jain DL, Baheti AM, Jain SR, Khandelwal KR. Use of medicinal plants among tribes in Satpuda region of Dhule and Jalgaon districts of Maharashtra – An ethnobotanical survey. Indian Journal of Traditional Knowledge 2010a; 9(1): 152-157.

18) Jain SP, Singh SC, Srivastava S, Singh J, Mishra NP, Prakash A. Hitherto unreported ethnomedicinal uses of plants of Betul district of Madhya Pradesh. Indian Journal of Traditional Knowledge 2010; 9(3): 522-525.

19) Jain SP, Srivastava S, Singh J, Singh SC. Traditional phytotherapy of Balaghat district, Madhya Pradesh, India. Indian Journal of Traditional Knowledge 2011; 10(2): 334-338.

20) Jain V. Sweets as traditional medicine in winter season: An ethnobotanical study in Udaipur city, India. Ethnobotany Research & Applications 2020; 20: 31.

21) Jeetendra S, Jeetendra P. Studies of ethnomedicinal plants used by tribals in some selected villages of Nimar region (M.P.). International Journal of Science and Research 2015; 4(2): 1206-1210.

22) Kadel C, Jain AK. Folklore claims on snakebite among some tribal communities of Central India. Indian Journal of Traditional Knowledge 2008; 7(2): 296-299.

23) Kala CP. Aboriginal uses and management of ethnobotanical species in deciduous forests of Chhattisgarh state in India. Journal of Ethnobiology and Ethnomedicine 2009; 5: 20.

24) Kala CP. Important gum yielding species *Anogeissus latifolia* (Roxb.) Bedd., *Boswellia serrata* Roxb. and *Sterculia urens* Roxb.: Ethnobotany, population density and management. Applied Ecology and Environmental Sciences 2016; 4(3): 61-65.

25) Kamble SY, More TN, Patil SR, Pawar SG, Bindurani R, Bodhankar SL. Plants used by the tribes of Northwest Maharashtra for the treatment of gastrointestinal disorders. Indian Journal of Traditional Knowledge 2008; 7(2): 321-325.

26) Kamble SY, Patil SR, Sawant PS, Sawant S, Pawar SG, Singh EA. Studies on plants used in traditional medicine by Bhilla tribe of Maharashtra. Indian Journal of Traditional Knowledge 2010; 9(3): 591-598.

27) Kamble SY, Sawant PS, Patil SR, Pawar SG, Singh EA. Traditional herbal remedies practiced by the herbal healers in the tribal regions of Maharashtra-India. International Journal of Life Sciences 2014; 2(4): 334-340.

28) Katekhaye SD, Bhutani KK. Standardization of a polyherbal Ayurvedic formulation: Ayaskrti. Indian Journal of Traditional Knowledge 2011; 10(4): 589-593.

29) Khonde VS, Kale MC, Badere RS. Ethnomedicinal survey of Armori, Wadsa, Kurkheda, Korchi forest range of Gadchiroli district, Maharashtra state, India. International Journal of Researches in Biosciences, Agriculture and Technology 2017; 4 (S2): 602-610.

30) Kshirsagar RD, Singh NP. Some Less Known Ethnomedicinal uses from Mysore and Coorg districts, Karnataka, Southern India. Ancient Science of Life 2001; 20: 20-25.

31) Kumar K, Abbas SG. Ethnomedicinal composition depends on floristic composition: A case studied in Sal forests of Jharkhand. International Journal of Pharmacy and Life Sciences 2012; 3(5): 1710-1719.

32) Kumar M, Bhatt V. Plant biodiversity and conservation of forests in foot hills of Garhwal Himalaya. Lyonia 2006; 11(2): 43-59.

33) Kumar NJI, Kumar RN, Patil N, Soni H. Studies on plant species used by tribal communities of Saputara and Purna forests, Dang district, Gujarat. Indian Journal of Traditional Knowledge 2007; 6(2): 368-374.

34) Kumar V, Sharma B. Gupteshwar Mahadev: A valuable sacred grove for conservation of medicinal flora in Parthapgah district, Rajasthan, India. Journal of Emerging Technologies and Innovative Research 2018; 5(4): 94-100.

35) Kumar V. Ethno-medicinal plants in five forest ranges in Dang's district, South Gujarat, India. Annals of Pharmacy and Pharmaceutical Sciences 2015; 6(1&2): 33-42.

36) Kuvar SD, Shinde RD. Plants used by Kokni tribe as antidote for snake bite and scorpion sting from Nasik and Dhule districts of Maharashtra. Journal of Global Biosciences 2019; 8(3): 6043-6050.

37) Lakshminarayana V, Rao NGM. Ethnoveterinary Practices in Northcoastal Districts of Andhra Pradesh, India. Journal of Natural Remedies 2013; 13(2): 109-117.

38) Marko BK, Sandya GS. Ethnobotanical study of traditional medicinal plants used by tribe of Dindori district (M.P.). International Journal of Applied Research 2020; 6(10): 90-93.

39) Meena KL, Dhaka V, Ahir PC. Traditional uses of ethnobotanical plants for construction of the Hut and hamlets in the Sitamata Wildlife Sanctuary of Rajasthan, India. Journal of Energy and Natural Resources 2013; 2(5): 33-40.

40) Meena KL, Yadav BL. Some ethnomedicinal plants used by the Garasia tribe of district Sirohi, Rajasthan. Indian Journal of Traditional Knowledge 2011; 10(2): 354-357.

41) Meena KL, Yadav BL. Some traditional ethnomedicinal plants of southern Rajasthan. Indian Journal of Traditional Knowledge 2010; 9(3): 471-474.

42) Meena KL. Some traditional ethno-veterinary plants ofdistrict Pratapgarh, Rajasthan, India. American Journal of Ethnomedicine 2014; 1(6): 393-401.

43) Mishra A. Study on some ethnomedicinal plants of Kalinjar hillock, Banda district (U.P) India. International Journal of Advanced Research in Engineering and Applied Sciences 2015a; 4(7): 1-9.

44) Mishra D. An ethnoveterinary survey of medicinal preparations used to treat painful delivery and retention of placenta in domestic cattle in Polasara block, Ganjam district, Odisha, India. Journal of Research in Biology 2015b; 5(2): 1659-1666.

45) Misra A. Vegetation Cover and Medidcinal Use of Chitraokoot Kamadgiri Hill Plants. International Journal of Bioinformatics and Biomedical Engineering 2015; 1(3): 216-221.

46) Murthy EN. Ethno medicinal plants used by gonds of Adilabad district, Andhra Pradesh, India. International Journal of Pharmacy and Life Sciences 2012; 3(10): 2034-2043.

47) Nair BMN, Punniamurthy N, Kumar SK. Ethno-veterinary Practices for Animal Health and the Associated Medicinal Plants from 24 Locations in 10 States of India. Research & Reviews: Journal of Veterinary Sciences 2017; 3(1): 25-34.

48) Nandini N, Shiddamallayya N. Potential minor forest products wealth of old Mysore district, Karnataka, India. International Journal of Current Innovation Research 2015; 1(5): 109-115.

49) Narayanan RMK, Mithunlal S, Sujanapal P, Kumar AN, Sivadasan M, Alfarhan AH, Alatar AA.Ethnobotanically important trees and their uses by Kattunaikka tribe in Wayanad Wildlife Sanctuary, Kerala, India. Journal of Medicinal Plants Research 2011; 5(4): 604-612.

50) Natarajan B, Paulsen BS. An ethnopharmacological study from Thane district, Maharashtra, India: Traditional knowledge compared with modern biological science. Pharmaceutical Biology 2000; 38(2): 139-151.

51) Orwa C, Mutua A, Kindt R , Jamnadass R, Anthony S. 2009 Agroforestree database: A tree reference and selection guide version 4.0 (http://apps.worldagroforestry.org/treedb/AFTPDFS/Anogeissus_latifolia. PDF)

52) Panda SK, Padhi L, Leyssen P, Liu M, Neyts J, Luyten W. Antimicrobial, anthelmintic, and antiviral activity of plants traditionally used for treating infectious disease in the Similipal Biosphere Reserve, Odisha, India. Frontiers in Pharmacology 2017; 8: 658.

53) Parijatham TR, Sujatha B, Lakshmi SB. Ethnomedicinal studies of medicinal plants in Eastern ghats of Vizianagaram district, Andhra Pradesh, India. International Journal of Bioassays 2016; 5(2): 4825-4842.

54) Patel R, Varshney A. Etheno-medicinal plant of Saputara Hill, Dang District, Gujarat. International Journal of Scientific Research and Management 2017; 5(9): 6965-6971.

55) Patil MV, Patil DA. Ethnomedicinal practices of Nasik district, Maharashtra. Indian Journal of Traditional Knowledge 2005; 4(3): 287-290.

56) Pradhan RN, Rautaraya O, Behera P, Panda SK. Diversity, medicinal uses and conservation status of medicinal plants at Mandaragiri, Angul forest division, Odisha, India. Natural Resources and Conservation 2014; 2(3): 43-50.

57) Punjani BL, Kumar V. Traditional medicinal plant remedies to treat cough and asthmatic disorders in the Aravalli ranges in North Gujarat, India. Journal of Natural Remedies 2002; 2: 173-178.

58) Ramakrishna N, Reddy ST, Sreelakshmi T, Sunitha EM, Saidulu C, Rajani A. Ethno-botanical survey in common plants of medicinal usage in tribal communities of Naikpods and Pardhan of different mandals of Adilabad district, Telangana state, India. International Journal of Innovative Pharmaceutical Sciences and Research 2015; 3(10): 1500-1512.

59) Rao SD, Rao BM, Murty PP, Venkaiah M. Ethnobotanical uses of certain plant species from Makkuva mandal, Vizianagaram distrct, Andhra Pradesh. International Journal of Current Research 2014; 6(3): 5387-5390.

60) Ratnam VK, Reddy TG, Raju VRR. Therapeutic importance of gums in folk medicine from Eastern Ghats, Andhra Pradesh. Asian Journal of Pharmaceutical and Clinical Research 2019; 12(7): 300-302.

61) Ravishankar B, Shukla VJ. Indian systems of medicine: a brief profile. African Journal of Traditional, Complementary and Alternative Medicine 2007; 4(3): 319-337.

62) Reddy ES, Kashinath BS. Traditional medical plants used for Piles and Fistula by Tribes of Mahur Taluka of Nanded District, Maharashtra, India. World Wide Journal of Multidisciplinary Research and Development 2016; 2(12): 34-36.

63) Reddy ES. Ethnomedicinal plants used for the treatment of respiratory disorders by rural and tribal communities in Mahur taluka of Nanded District, Maharashtra, India. International Journal for Innovative Research in Multidisciplinary Field 2017; 3(1): 40-44.

64) Reddy KN, Reddy CS, Raju VS. Ethnomedicinal Observations among the Kondareddis of Khammam District, Andhra Pradesh, India. Ethnobotanical Leaflets 2008; 12: 916-926.

65) Reddy KN, Subbaraju GV, Reddy CS, Raju VS. Ethnoveterinary medicine for treating livestock in eastern Ghats of Andhra Pradesh. Indian Journal of Traditional Knowledge 2006; 5(3): 368-372.

66) Reddy VRK, Devamma NM, Murty PP. Ethnoveterinary medicinal practices in Rayala seema regions of Andhra Pradesh, India. European Journal of Environmental Ecology 2016; 3(1): 7-20.

67) Reddy VRK, Devamma NM, Murty PP. Some folk medicinal plants of Bhiravakona hills of Prakasam district, A. P., India. Current Botany 2012; 3(5): 51-58.

68) Sabar B. Traditional Ecological Knowledge, Livelihood Options and Conservation Strategies among Chuktia Bhunjia tribe of Orissa, India. Journal of Biodiversity and Ecological Sciences 2014; 4(2): 73-88.

69) Saganuwan SA. Ethnoveterinary values of Nigerian medicinal plants: An overview. European Journal of Medicinal Plants 2017; 18(4): 1-35.

70) Sahu CR, Nayak RK, Dhal NK. The plant wealth of Boudh district of Odisha, India with reference to Ethnobotany. International Journal of Current Biotechnology 2013; 1(6): 4-10.

71) Samar R, Shrivastava PN, Jain M. Ethnobotanical study of traditional medicinal plants used by tribe of Guna district, Madhya Pradesh, India. International Journal of Current Microbiology and Applied Sciences 2015; 4(7): 466-471.

72) Sen S, Chakraborty R. Revival, modernization and integration of Indian traditional herbal medicine in clinical practice: Importance, challenges and future. Journal of Traditional and Complementary Medicine 2016; 7(2): 234-244.

73) Shankar R, Lale SK, Mudalya RK. Conservation and sustainable utilization of medicinal plants of Chandauli and Obra forests of Uttar Pradesh. Journal of Drug Research in Ayurvedic Sciences 2017; 2(2): 49-63.

74) Shankar R, Mudaiya RK, Lale SK, Gaur SK, Dhiman KS. Exploration, conservation and cultivation of medicinal plants in Balrampur, Gonda and Shravasti, districts of Uttar Pradesh. World Journal of Pharmaceutical Research 2016; 5(10): 549-571.

75) Sharma PP, Majumdar AM. Traditional knowledge on plants from Toranmal plateau of Maharashtra. Indian Journal of Traditional Knowledge 2003; 2(3): 292-296.

76) Shrivastava S, Kanungo VK. Ethnobotanical Survey of Surguja District with Special Reference to Plants Used by Uraon Tribe in Treatment of Diabetes. International Journal of Herbal Medicine 2013; 1 (3): 127-130.

77) Shukla AN, Srivastava S, Rawat AKS. An ethnobotanical study of medicinal plants of Rewa district, Madhya Pradesh. Indian Journal of Traditional Knowledge 2010; 9(1): 191-2020.

78) Singh GK, Ahirwar RK. Phyto-diversity of Ethnomedicinal plants of Chanda forest range district Dindori, Madhya Pradesh. International Journal of Life Sciences 2018; 6(1): 213-216.

79) Singh J, Meena KL. Medicinal Plants Used for Sexual Debility and Birth Control in Mandal Tehsil, Bhilwara, Rajasthan, India. Asian Resonance 2018; 7(3): 146-151.

80) Sivaraj N, Pandravada SR, Venkateswaran K, Dikshit N. Ethnic medicinal plant wealth of eastern Ghats: Status, knowledge systems and conservation strategies. International Journal of Current Research in Biosciences and Plant Biology 2017; 4(1): 83-101.

81) Sundaram SS, Suresh K. Potential of medicinal plants for curing human ailments in Natham, Dindigul district, Tamil Nadu, India. The Pharma Innovation 2019; 8(4): 512-514.

82) Thomas B, Mathews RP, Rajendran A, Kumar PKM. Ethnobotanical observations on tribe Arnatans of Nilambur Forest, Western Ghats region of Kerala, India. Research in Plant Biology 2013; 3(2): 12-17.

83) Upadhyay B, Singh KP, Kumar A. Ethno-veterinary uses and informants consensus factor of medicinal plants of Sariska region, Rajasthan, India. Journal of Ethnopharmacology 2011; 133: 14-25.

84) Vaidya AD, Devasagayam TP. Current status of herbal drugs in India: an overview. Journal of Clinical Biochemistry and Nutrition 2007; 41(1): 1-11.

85) Yadav R, Singh S, Kumar S, Dwivedi KN. A recent update on phytochemistry, pharmacology and medicinal value of axle wood (*Anogeissus latifolia* Wall. Cat). International Journal of Ayurveda and Pharmaceutical Chemistry 2017; 7(3): 197-205.

Cite this chapter as:

Mahalakshmi SN, Kekuda PTR. An inclusive review on ethnobotanical uses of *Anogeissus latifolia* (Combretaceae) in India. In: Kekuda PTR, Vinayaka KS, Raghavendra HL (Editors), Nature and Medicine: Traditional uses, chemistry and bioprospecting of natural products. JPS Scientific Publications, Tamil Nadu, India, 2020, Pp 38 - 50.

Nature and Medicine: Traditional Uses, Chemistry and Bioprocessing of Natural Products
ISBN: 978-81-947154-3-6
First Edition; 2020
Chapter – 5, Page: 51 - 59

5

A REVIEW ON ETHNOBOTANICAL USES OF *Ardisia solanacea* (Poir.) Roxb. (Primulaceae)

Rithu R, Rakshitha M.G and Prashith Kekuda T.R*

Department of Microbiology, S.R.N.M.N College of Applied Sciences, NES Campus, Balraj Urs road, Shivamogga – 577 201, Karnataka, India

*Corresponding author: p.kekuda@gmail.com

Abstract

Plants find several ethnobotanical uses such as food, fuel, cloth, flavor, and medicine. Many plant species have been widely used for primary health care especially in under-developed, developing countries. *Ardisia solanacea* is one of the important medicinal plants of the family Primulaceae. In this mini review, we report ethnobotanical uses of *A. solanacea*. The leaves and fruits of the plant are edible and are eaten raw or as vegetable. Parts *viz.*, leaves, stem, root, fruit and seeds of *A. solanacea* have ethnomedicinal significance. The plant is traditionally used to treat conditions such as boils, headache, indigestion, chest pain, cough, and gastrointestinal troubles. There is a great need for conservation of this plant species for its use in traditional medicine. The plant can be used to develop formulations that can be used to treat several ailments or disease conditions.

Key words: *Ardisia solanacea*, Traditional medicine, Ethnobotanical and Edible.

1. Introduction

Plants have been extensively utilized for various needs of man such as food, fuel wood, spices, and medicine. Indigenous medicinal systems all over the world use many plant species for treating several diseases and conditions such as diabetes, tuberculosis, cough, cold, urinary troubles, snake bite, skin diseases, bone fracture, diarrhea, dysentery, headache, viral infections, and inflammation and also for veterinary applications. According to WHO, majority of population in the world rely on the plants as sources of medicines. Plant based medicines are the only sources of primary health care for people living in remote places in several parts of the world. Nowadays, herbal medicine is gaining popularity in developed countries also. Besides medicinal applications, plants are also important with respect to ritual and spiritual belief in some traditions. Also, the medicinal plants have been a source of income for some communities (Hebbar *et al.*, 2004; Uniyal and Shiva, 2005; Sikarwar *et al.*, 2018; Bhat *et al.*, 2013; Hong *et al.*, 2015; Dey *et al.*, 2017; Gao *et al.*, 2019; Taram *et al.*, 2020).

2. *Ardisia solanacea* (POIR.) ROXB.

The genus *Ardisia* belongs to Primulaceae family of Angiosperms. The species of *Ardisia* are distributed in tropical and subtropical regions of the world and several species have food, ornamental and medicinal applications. *Ardisia* species contain several bioactive principles (Kobayashi and deMejia, 2005; Chang *et al.*, 2009; Chang *et al.*, 2011; Mu *et al.*, 2019). *Ardisia* species have been used worldwide for various ethnomedicinal and other traditional uses (Sawian *et al.*, 2007; Samuel *et al.*, 2010; Rahmatullah *et al.*, 2010; Rai and Lalramnghinglova, 2011; Ong *et al.*, 2011; Hong *et al.*, 2015a; Hong *et al.*, 2015b; Nurfadilah *et al.*, 2017; Nongmaithemand and Das, 2018; Reimers *et al.*, 2019; Gao *et al.*, 2019). One of the medicinally important species of the genus *Ardisia* is *Ardisia solanacea* (Poir.) Roxb. *A. solanacea* is a small to medium sized shrub or tree with simple and alternate leaves. The flowers are bright pink, in axillary or lateral umbels. The fruit of *A. solanacea* is a berry. It is an edible fruit plant with medicinal importance and is used as a source of dye (Thapa *et al.*, 2014; Jan *et al.*, 2018). The plant is also used in rituals (Franco and Narasimhan, 2009). In this mini review, we provide details on various ethnobotanical uses of *A. solanacea*.

3. Ethnomedicinal uses of *A. solanacea*

Many studies have shown that different parts viz. root, leaf, stem, seed and fruit of *A. solanacea* possess medicinal importance and are used by several tribal communities and indigenous medicinal systems to treat various diseases or ailments

such as boils, asthma, dysentery, chest pain, eye pain, blood clot, hemorrhage and headache. A brief description on the medicinal importance of *A. solanacea* is presented in Table - 1.

Table 1: Medicinal uses of *Ardisia solanacea*

Area	Plant part	Uses	References
Sundergarh district, Odisha, India	Root	Blood dysentery	Mallick and Mahana (2018)
Chittagong Hill Tracts, Bangladesh	Leaf	Boils	Morshed (2013)
Nawarangpur district, Odisha, India	Root	Asthma	Dhal *et al.* (1015)
Greater Khulna division, Bangladesh	Leaf and fruit	Colic	Rahmatullah *et al.* (2010)
Car Nicobar Island, India	Leaf	Abortion	Verma *et al.* (2010)
Andaman Islands, India	Leaf	Chest pain	Sharief (2007)
Chota Nagpur plateau, India	Stem	Pain in head	Dey *et al.* (2017)
Dehradun, Uttarakhand, India	Root	Indigestion	Jan *et al.* (2018)
Southern Odisha, India	Fruit	Used as medicine	Misra & Misra (2016)
Adilabad district, Andhra Pradesh, India	Tender tips	Cough	Ramakrishna and Saidulu (2014)
Madhya Pradesh, India	Seed	Gastrointestinal problems	Rai (2012)
Hill tract districts, Bangladesh	Leaf	Boils	Rahman *et al.* (2007)
Great Nicobar Island, India	Root	Blood clot, internal hemorrhage	Arora (2010)
Orissa, India	Fruit	Fits, eye pain	Franco and Narasimhan (2009)
Wayanad district, Kerala, India	Bark	Tooth ache	Prasad and Shyma (2013)
Visakhapatnam district, Andhra Pradesh, India	Leaf	Pain	Padal *et al.* (2010)
Chittagong hill tracts, Bangladesh	Root-bark	Sores	Brishty *et al.* (2020)
Wayanad district, Kerala, India	Root	Acidity	Prasad *et al.* (2013)
Koraput, Odisha, India	Fruit	Cuts and wounds	Mishra *et al.* (2016)
Ajoydha Hill region, Purulia district, India	Stem-bark	Headache	Dey and De (2010)
Jalpaiguri, West Bengal, India	Root	Fever, rheumatism, diarrhea	Saha *et al.* (2013)
Eastern Ghats of Andhra Pradesh, India	Stem	Whooping cough	Reddy *et al.* (2006)
Palakkad district, Kerala, India	Leaf	Medicine	Ramesh *et al.* (2016)
Wayanad district, Kerala, India	Leaf	Gout, mental disorder, diarrhea, vertigo, dysmenorrhea, rheumatic arthritis, skin sore	Shijad and Khaleel (2020)
Rangamati and Khagrachari Hill District, Bangladesh	Leaf	Boils	Paul *et al.* (2019)
Central Western Ghats, Karnataka, India	Root	Skin disease	Bhat *et al.* (2014)
Uttar Pradesh, India	Root	Diarrhea	Shukla *et al.* (2013)

4. Edible and other Ethnobotanical uses of *A. solanacea*

Apart from medicinal uses, *A. solanacea* is also important as leaves and fruits of the plant are edible and are consumed in many places. The plant is used as fuel wood, fodder and also used ritually in some area. Table - 2 provide some details on ethnobotanical uses of *A. solanacea* other than medicinal uses.

Table - 2: Food and other uses of *A. solanacea*

Area	Part	Uses	References
Andhra Pradesh, India	Leaf	Used as vegetable	Reddy *et al.* (2007)
Eastern Himalaya, India	Leaf	Young leaves are edible	Taram *et al.* (2020)
Dehradun, Uttarakhand, India	Root	Source of dye	Jan *et al.* (2018)
Southern Odisha, India	Fruit	Juice is prepared from fruits and consumed	Misra and Misra (2016)
Western Nepal	Fruit	Edible	Thapa *et al.* (2014)
Great Nicobar Island, India	Fruit	Edible	Arora (2010)
Meghalaya, India	Fruit	Edible	Singh *et al.* (2012)
Orissa, India	Fruit	Edible	Franco and Narasimhan (2009)
Orissa, India	Leaf	Vegetable	Franco and Narasimhan (2009)
Orissa, India	Leaf	Ritual	Franco and Narasimhan (2009)
Dudhwala National Park, India	Fruit	Edible	Rajesh *et al.* (2013)
Palakkad district, Kerala, India	Leaf	Edible	Ramesh *et al.* (2016)
Great Nicobar Island, India	Fruit and leaf	Edible	Sharief and Rao (2007)
Changlang district, Arunachal Pradesh, India	Fruit	Edible	Lungphi *et al.* (2018)
Kuldiha wildlife sanctuary, Odisha, India	Flower	Edible	Saravanan *et al.* (2020)
Dhading district, Central Nepal	Fruit	Fruits are edible; plant is used as fodder and fuel wood	Kunwar et al. (2006)

5. Conclusions

An in-detail literature survey on ethnobotanical uses of *A. solanacea* revealed its food, ritual and ethnomedicinal application in different indigenous systems of medicine. *A. solanacea* is widely used in traditional medicine in India. The edible as well as the medicinal uses highlights the possible utilization of the plant in therapy against various diseases. There is need for conservation of the plant species especially by tribal communities in order to meet healthcare. The plant may be explored in detail for bioactive metabolites for various pharmacological properties.

6. References

1) Arora K. Sustainable management of tropical forest through indigenous knowledge: A case study of Shompens of Great Nicobar Island. Indian Journal of Traditional Knowledge 2010; 9(3): 551-561.

2) Bhat JA, Kumar M, Bussmann RW. Ecological status and traditional knowledge of medicinal plants in Kedarnath Wildlife Sanctuary of Garhwal Himalaya, India. Journal of Ethnobiology and Ethnomedicine 2013; 9: 1.

3) Bhat P, Hegde GR, Hegde G, Mulgund GS. Ethnomedicinal plants to cure skin diseases - An account of the traditional knowledge in the coastal parts of Central Western Ghats, Karnataka, India. Journal of Ethnopharmacology 2014; 151: 493-502.

4) Brishty SR, Setu NI, Anwar MR, Jahan R, Mia MMK, Kadir MF, Islam MR. Ethnobotanical study on medicinal plants for dermatological disorders at Chittagong Hill Tracts, Bangladesh. Pharmaceutical and Biomedical Research 2020; 6(1): 61-90.

5) Chang CP, Chang HS, Peng CF, Lee SJ, Chen IS. Antitubercular resorcinol analogs and benzenoid C-glucoside from the roots of *Ardisia cornudentata*. Planta Medica 2011; 77(1): 60-65.

6) Chang HS, Lin YJ, Lee SJ, Yang CW, Lin WY, Tsai IL, Chen IS. Cytotoxic alkyl benzoquinones and alkyl phenols from *Ardisia virens*. Phytochemistry 2009; 70(17-18): 2064-2071.

7) Dey A, De JN. A survey of ethnomedicinal plants used by the tribals of Ajoydha Hill region, Purulia district, India. American-Eurasian Journal of Sustainable Agriculture 2010; 4(3): 280-290.

8) Dey A, Gorai P, Mukherjee A, Dhan R, Modak BK. Ethnobiological treatments of neurological conditions in the Chota Nagpur Plateau, India. Journal of Ethnopharmacology 2017; 198: 33-44.

9) Dhal NK, Panda SS, Muduli SD. Traditional uses of medicinal plants by native people in Nawarangpur district, Odisha, India. Asian Journal of Plant Science and Research 2015; 5(2): 27-33.

10) Franco MF, Narasimhan D. Plant names and uses as indicators of knowledge patterns. Indian Journal of Traditional Knowledge 2009; 8(4): 645-648.

11) Gao L, Wei N, Yang G, Zhang Z, Liu G, Cai C. Ethnomedicine study on traditional medicinal plants in the Wuliang Mountains of Jingdong, Yunnan, China. Journal of Ethnobiology and Ethnomedicine 2019; 15: 41.

12) Hebbar SS, Harsha VH, Shripathi V, Hegde GR. Ethnomedicine of Dharwad district in Karnataka, India--plants used in oral health care. Journal of Ethnopharmacology 2004; 94(2-3): 261-266.

13) Hong L, Guo Z, Huang Z, Wei S, Liu B, Meng S, Long C. Ethnobotanical study on medicinal plants used by Maonan people in China. Journal of Ethnobiology and Ethnomedicine 2015a; 11: 32.

14) Hong L, Zhuo J, Lei Q, Zhou J, Ahmed S, Wang C, Long Y, Li F, Long C. Ethnobotany of wild plants used for starting fermented beverages in Shui communities of southwest China. Journal of Ethnobiology and Ethnomedicine 2015b; 11: 42.

15) Jan M, Mir TA, Dhyani S. Ethnobotanical Study of plants used by ethnic people of Karbari Grant village Dehradun, Uttarakhand. SERBD-International Journal of Multidisciplinary Sciences 2018; 1(3): 1-6.

16) Karuppusamy S, Rajasekaran KM, Karmegam N. Evaluation of phytomedicines from street herbal vendors in Tamil Nadu, South India. Indian Journal of Traditional Knowledge 2002; 1(1): 26-39.

17) Kobayashi H, de Mejía E. The genus Ardisia: a novel source of health-promoting compounds and phytopharmaceuticals. Journal of Ethnopharmacology 2005; 96(3): 347-354.

18) Kumar R, Singh MK, Avinash BK. Ethnobotany of Tharus of Dudhwa national park, India. Mintage Journal of Pharmaceutical & Medical Sciences 2013; 2(1): 6-11.

19) Kunwar RM, Nepal BK, Sigdel KP, Balami N. Contribution to the Ethnobotany of Dhading District, Central Nepal. Nepal Journal of Science and Technology 2006; 7: 65-69.

20) Lungphi P, Wangpan T, Tangjang S. Wild edible plants and their additional uses by the Tangsa community living in the Changlang district of Arunachal Pradesh, India. Pleione 2018; 12(2): 151-164.

21) Mallick SN, Mahana A. A survey of ethnomedicinal plants used by the paudi bhuiyan tribals of adjoining areas of Khandadhar waterfall, Bonai subdivision of Sundergarh district, Odisha, India. International Journal of Biology Research 2018; 3(2): 11-16.

22) Mishra M, Sujana KA, Dhole PA. Ethnomedicinal plants used for the treatment of cuts and wounds by tribes of Koraput in Odisha, India. Indian Journal of Plant Sciences 2016; 5(4): 14-19.

23) Misra S, Misra MK. Ethnobotanical and nutritional evaluation of some edible fruit plants of Southern Odisha, India. International Journal of Advances in Agricultural Science and Technology 2016; 3(1): 1-30.

24) Morshed AJM. A Survey of Medicinal Plants as Regards to their Uses by the Tribal Practitioners in the Chittagong Hill Tracts of Bangladesh to Check Various Diseases. Hamdard Medicus 2013; 56(3): 18-40.

25) Mu LH, Yan H, Wang YN, Yu TF, Liu P. Triterpenoid saponins from *Ardisia gigantifolia* and mechanism on inhibiting proliferation of MDA-MB-231 cells. Biological and Pharmaceutical Bulletin 2019; 42(2): 194-200.

26) Nongmaithemand R, Das AK. Quantitative ethnobotanical documentation of the medicinal plants used by the indigenous Maring tribe of Chandel district of Manipur, India. International Journal of Advanced Research 2018; 6(2): 883-898.

27) Nurfadilah S, Hapsari L, Abywijaya IK.Species richness, conservation status, and potential uses of plants in Segara Anakan Area of Sempu Island, East Java, Indonesia. Biodiversitas 2017; 18(4): 1568-1588.

28) Ong HC, Ruzalila BN, Milow P. Traditional knowledge of medicinal plants among the Malay villagers in Kampung Tanjung Sabtu, Terengganu, Malaysia. Indian Journal of Traditional Knowledge 2011; 10(3): 460-465.

29) Padal SB, Murty PP, Rao SD, Venkaiah M. Ethnomedicinal plants from Paderu division of Visakhapatnam district, A.P, India. Journal of Phytology 2010; 2(8): 70-91.

30) Paul AK, Alam MJ, Alam JAHM. A preliminary survey of ethno-medicinal plants used by the Chakma community of Rangamati and Khagrachari Hill District, Bangladesh. Arabian Journal of Medicinal & Aromatic Plants 2019; 5(2): 1-22.

31) Prasad DAG, Shyma TB, Raghavendra MP. Plants used by the tribes for the treatment of digestive system disorders in Wayanad district, Kerala. Journal of Applied Pharmaceutical Science 2013; 3(8): 171-175.

32) Prasad DAG, Shyma TB. Medicinal plants used by the tribes of Vythiri taluk, Wayanad district (Kerala state) for the treatment of human and domestic animal ailments. Journal of Medicinal Plants Research 2013; 7(20): 1439-1451.

33) Rahman MA, Uddin SB, Wilcock CC. Medicinal plants used by Chakma tribe in Hill tracts districts of Bangladesh. Indian Journal of Traditional Knowledge 2007; 6(3): 508-517.

34) Rai PK, Lalramnghinglova H. Ethnomedicinal plants of India with special reference to an Indo-Burma hotspot region: An overview. Ethnobotany Research and Applications 2011; 9: 379-420.

35) Rai R. Ethnobotanical studies on Korku tribes of Madhya Pradesh. Forestry Bulletin 2012; 12(2): 86-93.

36) Rahmatullah M, Mollik MAH, Paul AK, Jahan R, Khatun MA, Seraj S, Chowdhury AR, Bashar ABMA, Wahab SMR, Taufiq-ur-Rahman M. A comparative analysis of medicinal plants used to treat gastrointestinal

disorders in two sub-districts of Greater Khulna division, Bangladesh. Advances in Natural and Applied Sciences 2010; 4(1): 22-28.

37) Ramakrishna N, Saidulu C. Medicinal plants used by ethnic people of Adilabad district, Andhra Pradesh, India. International Journal of Pharmaceutical Research and Allied Sciences 2014; 3(2): 51-59.

38) Ramesh M, Manilal KS, Kumar MMS. Ethnobotanical aspects of trees of Palakkad District, Kerala, India. Devagiri Journal of Science 2016; 2(1): 32-51.

39) Reddy KN, Reddy CS, Trimurthulu G. Ethnobotanical Survey on Respiratory Disorders in Eastern Ghats of Andhra Pradesh, India†. Ethnobotanical Leaflets 2006; 10: 139-148.

40) Reimers EAL, Fernández EC, Reimers DJL, Chaloupkova P, Del Valle JMZ, Milella L, Russo D. An Ethnobotanical Survey of Medicinal Plants Used in Papantla, Veracruz, Mexico. Plants (Basel) 2019; 8(8): 246.

41) Saha G, Biswas R, Das AP. Survey of medicinal plants in the Gorumara National Park, Jalpaiguri, West Bengal, India. Pleione 2013; 7(1): 127-137.

42) Samuel AJSJ, Kalusalingam A, Chellappan DK, Gopinath R, Radhamani S, Husain HA, Muruganandham V, Promwichit P. Ethnomedical survey of plants used by the Orang Asli in Kampung Bawong, Perak, West Malaysia. Journal of Ethnobiology and Ethnomedicine 2010; 6: 5.

43) Saravanan R, Kannan D, Panda SP, Datta S. Traditionally used wild edible plants of Kuldiha wildlife sanctuary (KWLS), Odisha, India. Journal of Pharmacognosy and Phytochemistry 2020; SP6: 482-488.

44) Sawian JT, Jeeva S, Lyndem FG, Mishra BP, Laloo RC. Wild edible plants of Meghalaya, North-east India. Natural Product Radiance 2007; 6(5): 410-426.

45) Sharief MU, Rao RR. Ethnobotanical studies of Shompens – A critically endangered and degenerating ethnic community in Great Nicobar Island. Current Science 2007; 93(11): 1623-1628.

46) Sharief MU. Plants folk medicine of Negrito tribes of Bay Islands. Indian Journal of Traditional Knowledge 2007; 6(3): 468-476.

47) Shijad MVM, Khaleel KM. Indigenous Knowledge of Medicinal Plants Used by the Tribes in Muthanga Range of Wayanad Wildlife Sanctuary, Wayanad, Kerala, India. International Journal of Botany Studies 2020; 5(2): 163-171.

48) Sikarwar RLS, Pathak B, Jaiswal A. Some unique ethnomedicinal preparations of tribal communities of Chitrakoot, Madhya Pradesh. Indian Journal of Traditional Knowledge 2008; 7(4): 613-617.

49) Singh B, Sinha BK, Phukan SJ, Borthakur SK, Singh VN. Wild edible plants used by Garo tribes of Nokrek biosphere reserve in Meghalaya, India. Indian Journal of Traditional Knowledge 2012; 11(1): 166-171.

50) Shukla AN, Srivastava S, Rawat AKS. A survey of Traditional medicinal plants of Uttar Pradesh (India) - Used in treatment of infectious diseases. Nature and Science 2013; 11(9): 24-36.

51) Taram M, Borah D, Mipun P, Taram V, Das AP. Evaluation of ethnobotanical knowledge in Komkar-Adi Biocultural Landscape of Eastern Himalayan Region of India. Asian Journal of Ethnobiology 2020; 3(2): 70-87.

52) Thapa LB, Dhakal TM, Chaudhary R. Wild edible plants used by endangered & indigenous Raji tribe in Western Nepal. International Journal of Applied Sciences and Biotechnology 2014; 2(3): 243-252.

53) Tsering J, Gogoi BJ, Hui PK, Tam N, Tag H. Ethnobotanical appraisal on wild edible plants used by the Monpa community of Arunachal Pradesh. Indian Journal of Traditional Knowledge 2017; 16(4): 626-637.

54) Uniyal B, Shiva V. Traditional Knowledge on medicinal plants among rural women of the Garhwal Himalaya, Uttaranchal. Indian Journal of Traditional Knowledge 2005; 4(3): 259-266.

55) Verma C, Bhatia S, Srivastava S. Traditional medicine of the Nicobarese. Indian Journal of Traditional Knowledge 2010; 9(4): 779-785.

Cite this chapter as:

Rithu R, Rakshitha MG, Kekuda PTR. Ethnobotanical uses of *Ardisia solanacea* (Poir.) Roxb. (Primulaceae) – A mini review. In: Kekuda PTR, Vinayaka KS, Raghavendra HL (Editors), Nature and Medicine: Traditional uses, chemistry and bioprospecting of natural products. JPS Scientific Publications, Tamil Nadu, India, 2020, Pp 50 - 59.

Nature and Medicine: Traditional Uses, Chemistry and Bioprocessing of Natural Products
ISBN: 978-81-947154-3-6
First Edition; 2020
Chapter – 6, Page: 60 - 72

6

BIOACTIVE COMPOUNDS FROM *Alangium salviifolium* (L.f.) Wangerin (Cornaceae) – A MINI REVIEW

Prashith Kekuda T. R[1], Mahalakshmi S. N[2*] and Chaithra M[3]

[1]Department of Microbiology, S.R.N.M.N College of Applied Sciences, NES Campus, Balraj Urs road, Shivamogga – 577 201, Karnataka, India
[2]Department of Zoology, S.R.N.M.N College of Applied Sciences, NES Campus, Balraj Urs road, Shivamogga – 577 201, Karnataka, India
[3]Department of Biochemistry, S.R.N.M.N College of Applied Sciences, NES Campus, Balraj Urs road, Shivamogga – 577 201, Karnataka, India

*Corresponding author: p.kekuda@gmail.com

Abstract

Alangium salviifolium (L.f.) Wangerin (Cornaceae) is one of the important plants having widespread medicinal uses and is commonly known as sage-leaved alangium. The plant is a bushy, small tree and is reported to contain a wide range of phytochemicals such as phenolic compounds, alkaloids, flavonoids, triterpenes and glycosides. An extensive literature survey on the plant revealed isolation of various compounds representing phytochemical groups such as alkaloids, flavonoids, tannins, glycosides, and terpenes from *A. salviifolium*. Studies have come out with the isolation and structural elucidation of several compounds belonging to alkaloids, terpenes and other groups. Many of these isolated constituents were shown to exhibit

biological activities viz. antidiabetic, cytotoxic, anti-inflammatory, pesticidal, antibacterial, enzyme inhibitory and antioxidant activities. In this review, we present details on phytochemicals detected in *A. salviifolium* and biological activities of some of the isolated chemical compounds.

Key words: *Alangium salviifolium*, Phytochemistry, Phytochemicals and Bioactive compounds

1. Introduction

Plants produce a variety of metabolites which are broadly classified into two groups *viz.*, primary metabolites and secondary metabolites. Most of these compounds are beneficial for plants as they protect plants from herbivorous animals and insects. Many compounds are responsible for fragrance and aroma of plants. The therapeutic potential of plants is due to the presence of several secondary metabolites present in the plants such as alkaloids, phenolic compounds and terpenes. In some cases, the presence of characteristic secondary metabolites in plants also helps in the identification of plant species. Morphine, vincristine, vinblastine, taxol, and quinine are few of the plant secondary metabolites having therapeutic potential. Plant secondary metabolites exert several pharmacological potential such as antimicrobial, antioxidant and anticancer activity (Cowan, 1999; Kasote *et al.*, 2015; Seca and Pinto, 2018). Bioanalytical techniques have been fruitful in the isolation and characterization of secondary metabolites in plants. Progress in chromatographic and spectral techniques lead to the discovery of several bioactive compounds in plants. Techniques such as thin layer chromatography, column chromatography, liquid chromatography-mass spectrometry, and nuclear magnetic resonance have been exploited for isolation and elucidation of structures of many phytochemicals (Hostettmann *et al.*, 1997; Wolfender *et al.*, 2001; Tran *et al.*, 2009; Marston and Hostettmann, 2009; Cai *et al.*, 2019).

Alangium salviifolium (L.f.) Wangerin [Synonym *Alangium lamarckii* Thw] (Figure - 1) is one of the important medicinal plants of the family Cornaceae and is commonly known as sage-leaved alangium in English and Ankole in Kannada. The plant is distributed in many countries including India. The plant is common in drier parts of India, in plains as well as in foothills of south India. Different part such as root, leaves, bark and fruits have got medicinal properties. Various parts of this plant are used in Ayurveda and in many tribal medicines (Khare, 2007; Shravya *et al.*, 2017; Patel and Manigauha, 2018). The plant is reported to exhibit a range of bioactivities such as antioxidant (Bhusari *et al.*, 2020), anthelmintic (Kochuthressia, 2018), antibacterial (Anjum *et al.*, 2002), antifungal (Panda *et al.*, 2017), anticancer (Zahan *et al.*, 2011), anti-inflammatory (Ahad *et al.*, 2012), hepatoprotective (Dhruve

et al., 2020), anti-arthritic (Jubie *et al.*, 2008), hypoglycemic (Ahad *et al.*, 2011), antifertility (Murugan *et al.*, 2000), antidepressant (Shashikumara *et al.*, 2017), antiepileptic (Sharma *et al.*, 2011), anticonvulsant (Sharma *et al.*, 2011), analgesic (Sharma *et al.*, 2011), insecticidal (Selin-Rani *et al.*, 2016), molluscicidal (Tanwer and Vijayvergia, 2012), antidiarrhoeal (Zahan *et al.*, 2012), wound healing (Inayathulla *et al.*, 2010), acetylcholinesterase inhibitory (Nasrullah *et al.*, 2017) activities. In this mini review, we present details on the biological activities of isolated compounds from *A. salviifolium*.

Figure - 1: *Alangium salviifolium* **(Photograph by Dr. Vinayaka)**

2. Phytochemical groups identified in *A. salviifolium*

The plant *A. salviifolium* is a repository of several chemical compounds belonging to different groups. Studies have shown the presence of various phytochemical groups such as alkaloids, steroids, glycosides, tannins, and flavonoids in *A. salviifolium*. A brief description on various phytochemical groups identified in different parts viz. seeds, leaves, flowers and roots of *A. salviifolium* is presented in Table 1.

Table - 1: Phytochemical groups identified in different parts of A. salviifolium

Part	Extract	Phytochemical identified	Reference
Seed	Alcohol	Steroids, alkaloids and glycosides	Bhusari *et al.* (2020)
Seed	Solvents	Alkaloids, glycosides, tannins flavonoids and phytosterols	Sharma *et al.* (2011)
Leaf	Methanol	Alkaloids, flavonoids, steroids, terpenoids, tannins, glycosides and phenols	Prathyusha (2018)
Leaf	Ethanol	Alkaloids, glycosides, tannins and flavonoids	Patel and Manigauha (2018)
Flower	Methanol	Tannin, flavonoid, phenol, steroid and alkaloid	Zahan *et al.* (2012)
Flower	Chloroform	Tannin, flavonoid, alkaloid, phenol and steroid	Nahar *et al.* (2012)
Root	Ethanol	Phytosterols, alkaloids, flavonoids and triterpenes	Ahad *et al.* (2011) and Ahad *et al.* 2012)
Bark	Methanol	Flavonoids, phenolic compounds, phytosterols, alkaloids, tannin and saponins	Rajkumar and Kumar (2011)
Root	Ethanol	Flavonoids, glycosides, alkaloids, terpenoids, tannins and saponins	Aphajal and Jaish (2019)

3. Chemical compounds isolated and identified in *A. salviifolium*

Studies have identified several compounds from *A. salviifolium*. Dasgupta (1965) isolated Ankorine, a crystalline phenolic alkaloid from leaves. Compounds *viz.*, Venoterpine, *dl*-salsoline and isocephaeline were recovered from *A. salviifolium* (Achari *et al.*, 1980). Two compounds viz. 1-Methyl-1H-pyrimidine-2,4-dione and 3-O-b-D-glucopyranosyl-(24b)-ethylcholesta5,22,25-triene were isolated from the flowers of *A. salviifolium* (Anjum *et al.*, 2002). From the leaves of *A. salviifolium*, three phenolic glycosides, Salviifoside A, B and C, in addition to salicin, kaempferol, and kaempferol 3-O-beta-d-glucopyranoside (Figure 2) were isolated (Tran *et al.*, 2009). Compounds *viz.*, alangiumkaloids A and B, 27-O-trans-caffeoylcylicodiscic acid, and β-D-glucopyranos-1-yl N-methylpyrrole-2-carboxylate, myriceric acid B, isoalangiside, alangiside, 3-O-demethyl-2-O-methylalangiside, and demethylalangiside (Figure 3) are reported from *A. salviifolium* (Pailee *et al.*, 2011). A novel cadinane-type sesquiterpenoid compound named as (-)-7, 8-dihydroxycalamenal (Figure 4) was isolated from root essential oil (Yagi *et al.*, 2014). Pailee *et al.* (2015) isolated twelve cardinane sesquiterpenes viz. alangenes A-G, mansonone H, mansonone E, mansonone G, dehydrooxoperezinone, and (S)-()-lacinilene C from dichloromethane extract of stems (Figure - 5). Di-demethoxyAlanginol (Figure 6), a compound from aerial parts of *A. salviifolium* was isolated from the ethanolic extract (Kalarani and Venkatesh, 2017). Cai *et al.* (2019) isolated two octahydro-protoberberine alkaloids *viz.*, alangiifoliumines A and B, and two new protoemetine derivatives *viz.*, alangiifoliumines C and D from the stems of *A. salviifolium* (Figure - 7). In a study, Zhou *et al.* (2018) isolated two compounds *viz.*, 8-hydroxyl-cepheline (a new cepheline type alkaloid) and $\Delta^{1',2'}$-deoxytubulosine from

fruits of *A. salviifolium* (Figure - 8). A compound identified as 2-isopropyl-6-methoxy chromone (Figure - 9) was isolated from aerial parts of *A. salvIifolium* (Ramani *et al.*, 2003). Angustinine, a new benzopyridoquinolizine alkaloid (Figure - 10) was isolated from methanol extract of root bark of *A. salviifolium* (Chakraborty and Mukhopadhyay, 2012). The study of Itoh *et al.* (2000) identified two new alkaloids *viz.*, 1',2'-dehydrotubulosine and alangine from the dried fruits.

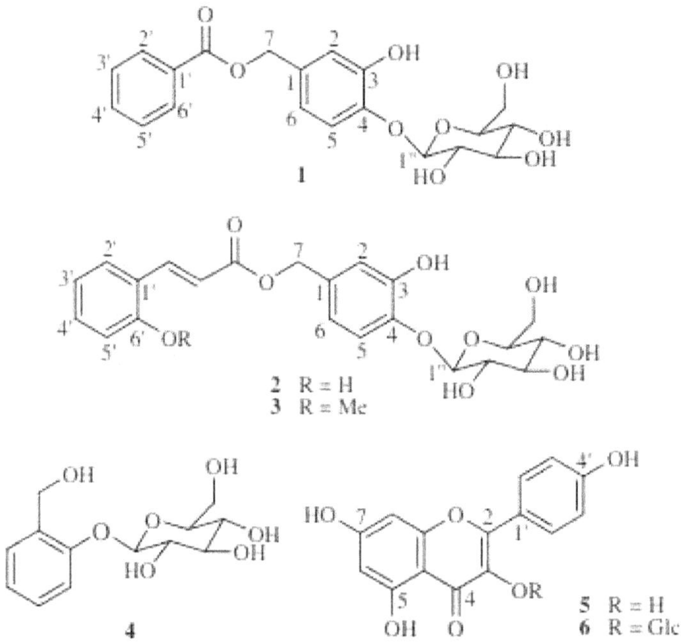

Figure - 2: Structures of Salviifosides AC (1, 2, 3), salicin (4), kaempferol (5), and kaempferol 3-O-b-D-glucopyranoside (6)

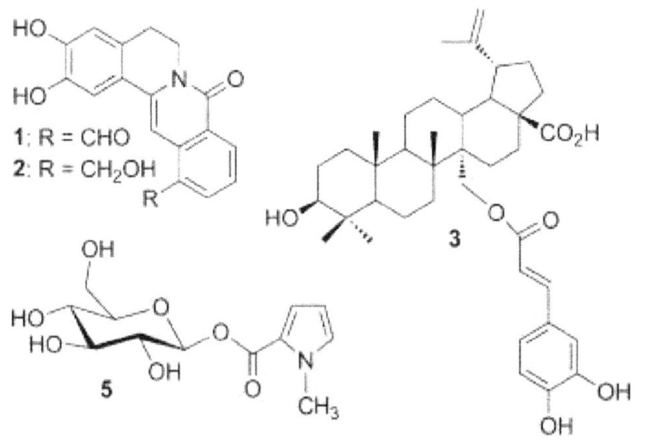

Figure - 3: Structures of alangiumkaloids A (1) and B (2), 27-O-trans-caffeoylcylicodiscic acid (3), and β-D-glucopyranos-1-yl N-methylpyrrole-2-carboxylate (5)

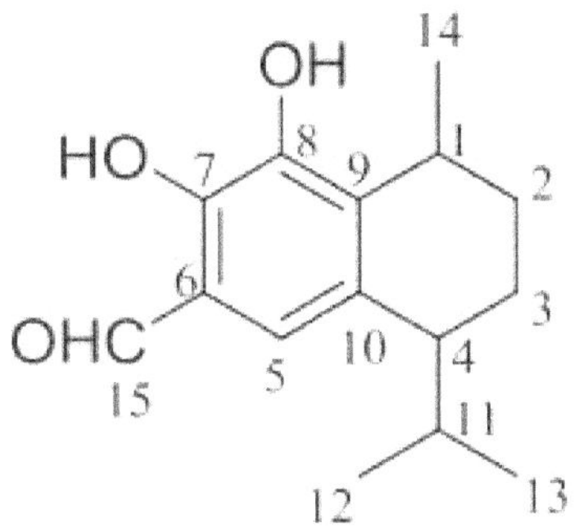

Figure - 4: Structure of (-)-7, 8-dihydroxycalamenal

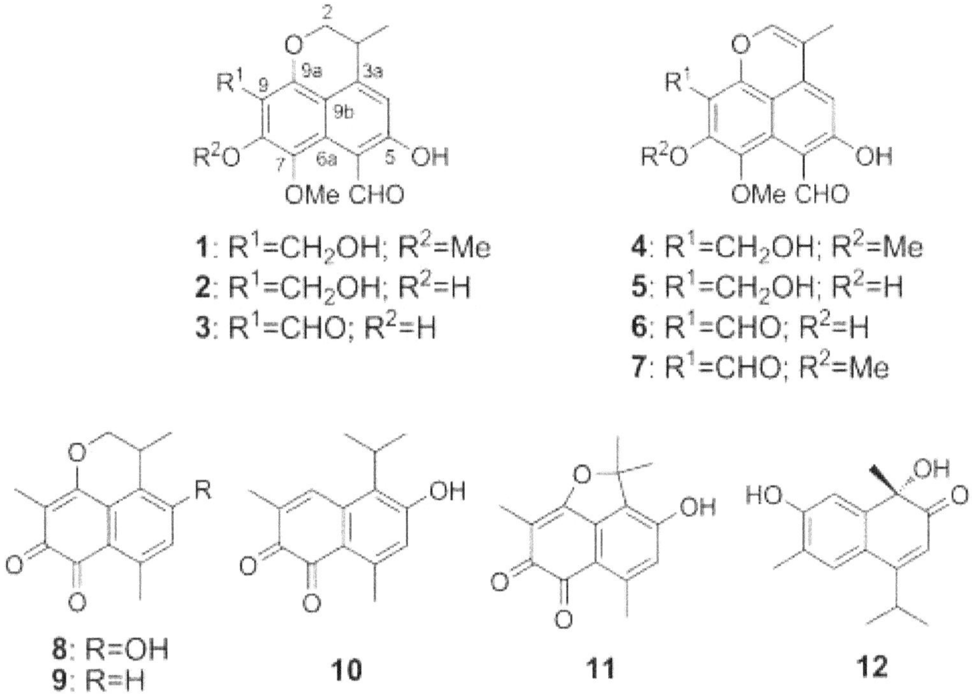

1: R¹=CH₂OH; R²=Me
2: R¹=CH₂OH; R²=H
3: R¹=CHO; R²=H

4: R¹=CH₂OH; R²=Me
5: R¹=CH₂OH; R²=H
6: R¹=CHO; R²=H
7: R¹=CHO; R²=Me

8: R=OH
9: R=H

10

11

12

Figure - 5: Structures of cardinane sesquiterpenes present in stems [Alangenes A-G (1–7), mansonone H (8), mansonone E (9), mansonone G (10), dehydrooxoperezinone (11), and (S)-()-lacinilene C (12)]

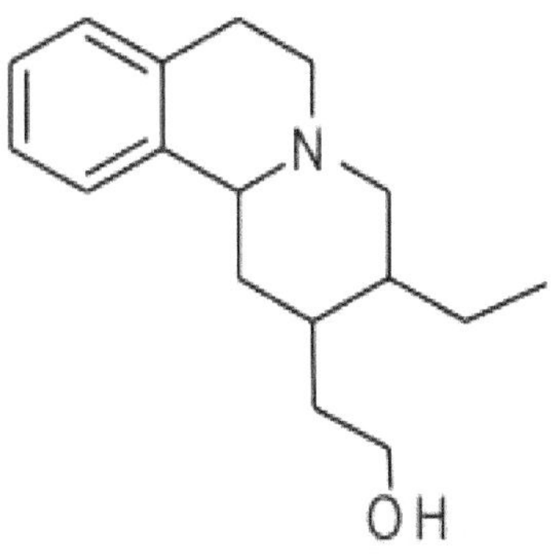

Figure - 6: Di-demethoxyAlanginol

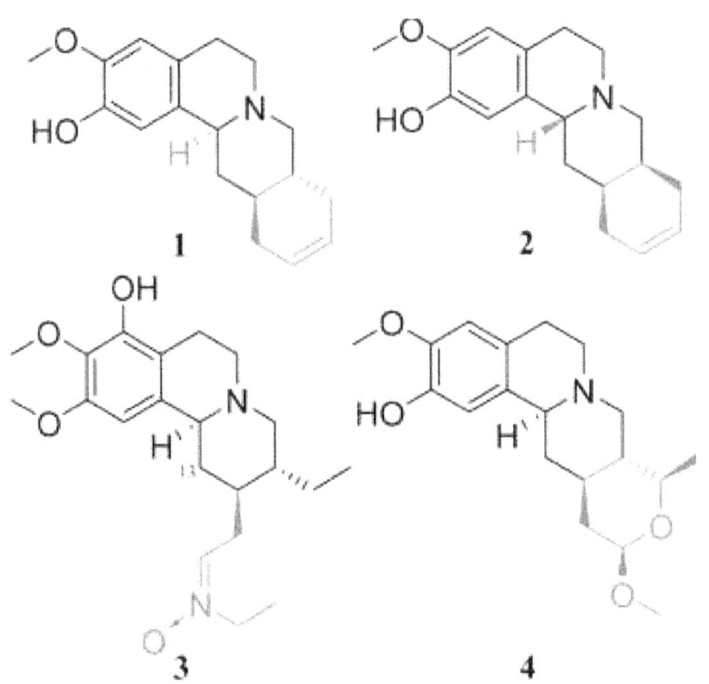

Figure - 7: Structures of octahydro-protoberberine alkaloids [Alangiifoliumines A (1) and B (2) and protoemetine derivatives, Alangiifoliumines C (3) and D (4)]

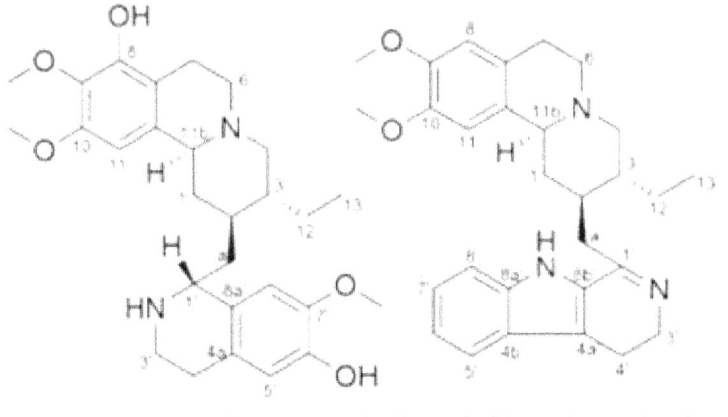

Figure - 8: Structures of 8-hydroxyl-cepheline (left) and Δ1',2'-deoxytubulosine (right)

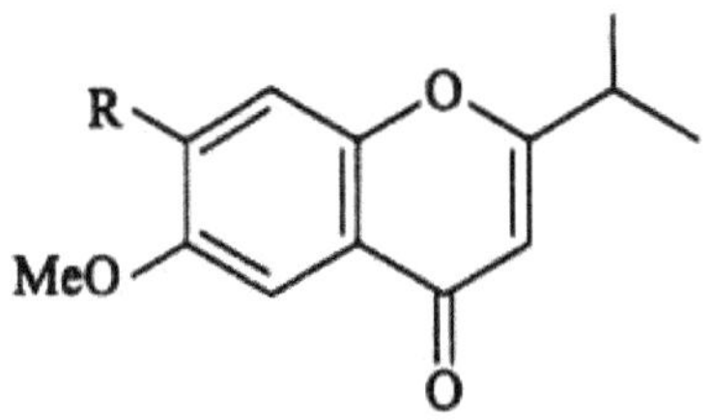

R=H: 2-isopropyl-6-methoxy chromone

Figure - 9: Structure of 2-isopropyl-6-methoxy chromone

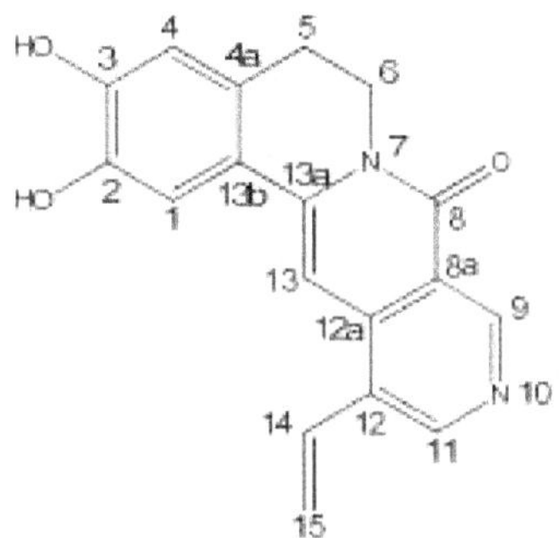

Figure - 10: Structure of Angustinine

4. Bioactivities of purified compounds from *A. salviifolium*

Studies have shown potent bioactivities such as antidiabetic, cytotoxic, antioxidant, enzyme inhibitory, pesticidal activities of compounds isolated from *A. salviifolium*. A brief description on bioactivities of purified compounds is presented here.

4.1. Antidiabetic activity

Two fractions FAS6 and FAS7 isolated from leaves and identified as flavonoid/phenolic compounds were shown to be effective antidiabetic agents significantly reduced the blood glucose level in STZ-induced diabetic rats as compared to the diabetic control group (Patel and Manigauha, 2018).

4.2. Pesticidal activity

Two fractions designated as F-IV and F-VI recovered from methanolic extract of *A. salviifolium* through chromatographic technique were shown to display concentration dependent pesticidal activity against 4th instar larvae of *Spodoptera litura* (Selin-Rani *et al.*, 2016).

4.3. Antioxidant activity

In a study, compounds viz. 27-O-trans-caffeoylcylicodiscic acid, myriceric acid B, and demethylalangiside isolated from *A. salviifolium* were shown to display scavenging activity against DPPH radicals with an IC_{50} value of 21.4, 21.8 and 24.0 µM, respectively. Alangiside and demethylalangiside showed inhibitory activity against superoxide anion radical formation with an IC_{50} values of 19.4 and 5.3 µM, respectively. Compounds *viz.*, isoalangiside, alangiside, 3-O-demethyl-2-O-methylalangiside, and demethylalangiside were effective in showing activity in ORAC assay (Pailee *et al.*, 2011). A compound designated as (-)-7, 8-dihydroxycalamenal was shown to display antioxidant activity in ORAC assay (Yagi *et al.*, 2014).

Chapter - 6

4.4. Enzyme inhibitory activity

Myriceric acid B and 27-O-trans-caffeoylcylicodiscic acid isolated from *A. salviifolium* showed inhibitory activity against aromatase activity with IC_{50} values of 6.8 and 4.7 µM, respectively (Pailee *et al.*, 2011). A novel cadinane-type sesquiterpenoid designated as (-)-7, 8-dihydroxycalamenal, isolated from root essential oil displayed inhibitory activity against tyrosinase (Yagi *et al.*, 2014).

4.5. Anti-inflammatory activity

In a study, Salviifoside B isolated from the leaves was shown to potentially inhibits the productions of nitric oxide, prostaglandin E(2), and tumor necrosis factor-alpha indicating potent anti-inflammatory activities in lipopolysaccharide-induced inflammation in murine macrophage cells line RAW 264.7 (Tran *et al.*, 2009).

4.6. Cytotoxic activity

Compounds *viz.*, Myriceric acid B and 27-O-trans-caffeoylcylicodiscic acid isolated from *A. salviifolium* exhibited cytotoxicity against MOLT-3 cells with an IC_{50} values of 3.9 and 5.6 µM, respectively. 3-O-demethyl-2-O-methylalangiside showed selective cytotoxicity against HepG2 cells with an IC_{50} value of 7.1µM (Pailee *et al.*, 2011). Four compounds *viz.*, alangenes A-D, isolated from stems of *A. salviifolium* displayed selective cytotoxicity against MOLT-3 cells (Pailee *et al.*, 2015). Two compounds viz. 8-hydroxyl-cepheline and $\Delta^{1',2'}$-deoxytubulosine isolated from fruits of *A. salviifolium* were effective in displaying cytotoxicity against cell lines HeLa, A-549 and SKOV-3 (Zhou *et al.*, 2018). Two alkaloids *viz.*, alangiifoliumine A and alangiifoliumine C were shown to display cytotoxic potential against A-549, HeLa, and SKOV-3 (Cai *et al.*, 2019).

4.7. Antibacterial activity

Two compounds *viz.*, 1-Methyl-1H-pyrimidine-2,4-dione and 3-O-b-D-glucopyranosyl-(24b)-ethylcholesta5,22,25-triene, isolated from the flowers were shown to display remarkable antibacterial activities against Gram-positive and Gram-negative bacterial species (Anjum *et al.*, 2002).

5. Conclusions

A detailed literature survey indicated that *A. salviifolium* contains a variety of phytochemicals and several compounds that have been characterized exhibit a range of bioactivities such as antibacterial, antioxidant, cytotoxic, antidiabetic and anti-inflammatory activities. The plant is a one of the well-known medicinal plants

containing several bioactive principles and can be screened in detail for developing novel drugs active against several diseases or ailments of humans.

Acknowledgements

Authors are thankful to Dr. Raghavendra H.L. Faculty of Medicine, The Medical School (FMB), Sao Paulo State University (UNESP), Botucatu-18618-687, Sao Paulo State, Brazil for providing some useful literatures.

6. References

1) Achari B, Ali E, Dastidar GPP, Sinha RR, Pakrashi SC. Further investigations on the alkaloids of *Alangium lamarckii*. Planta Medica 1980; 40: 5-7

2) Ahad HA, Padmaja BS, Sravanthi M, Ramyasree P, Kavitha K. Phytochemical screening and anti-inflammatory actions of *Alangium salviifolium* root extract. Natural Product Research 2012; 26(17): 1649-1653.

3) Ahad HA, Padmaja BS, Yesupadam P, Guruprakash P, Sravanthi M, Ramyasree P. Phytochemical and hypoglycaemic evaluation of *Alangium salvifolium* root extract. Journal of Scientific Research 2011; 3(2): 393-402.

4) Anjum A, Ekramul Haque M, Mukhlesur Rahman M, Sarker SD. Antibacterial compounds from the flowers of *Alangium salviifolium*. Fitoterapia 2002; 73(6): 526-528.

5) Aphajal M, Jaish BM. Phytochemical screening of *Alangium salviifolium* (L.f.) Wangerin showing antifungal properties against *Alternaria* spp. Plantae Scientia 2019; 2(1): 1-4.

6) Bhusari S, Waghmare S, Nikam K, Wakte P. In-vitro anti-oxidant activity and free radical scavenging potential of *Alangium salvifolium* seeds. Research Journal of Pharmacy and Technology 2020; 13(7): 3081-3085.

7) Cai YS, Wang C, Tian C, Sun WT, Chen L, Xiao D, Zhou SY, Qiu G, Yu J, Zhu K, Yang SP. Octahydro-Protoberberine and Protoemetine-type alkaloids from the stems of *Alangium salviifolium* and their cytotoxicity. Journal of Natural Products 2019 27; 82(9): 2645-2652.

8) Chakraborty M, Mukhopadhyay S. Angustinine – A new benzopyridoquinolizine alkaloid from *Alangium lamarckii*. Natural Product Communications 2012; 7(9): 1169-1170.

9) Cowan MM. Plant products as antimicrobial agents. Clinical Microbiology Reviews 1999; 12(4): 564-582.

10) Dasgupta B. Chemical investigations of *Alangiun lamarckii* I. Isolation of a new alkaloid, Ankorine, from the leaves. Journal of Pharmaceutical Analysis 1965; 54(3): 481-483.

Chapter - 6

11) Dhruve P, Nauman M, Kale RK, Singh RP. A novel hepatoprotective activity of *Alangium salviifolium* in mouse model. Drug and Chemical Toxicology 2020: 1-13.

12) Hostettmann K, Wolfender JL, Rodriguez S. Rapid detection and subsequent isolation of bioactive constituents of crude plant extracts. Planta Medica 1997; 63(1): 2-10.

13) Inayathulla, Karigar AA, Shariff WR, Sikarwar MS. Wound healing property of alcoholic extract of leaves of *Alangium salvifolium*. Journal of Pharmacy Research 2010; 3(2): 267-269.

14) Itoh A, Ikuta Y, Tanahashi T. Nagakuara N. Two Alangium alkaloids from *Alangium lamarckii*. Journal of Natural Products 2000; 63: 723-725.

15) Jubie S, Jawahar N, Koshy R, Gowramma B, Murugan V, Suresh B. Anti-arthritic activity of bark extracts of *Alangium salviifolium* Wang. Rasayan Journal of Chemistry 2008; 1(3): 433-436.

16) Kalarani HD, Venkatesh P. Isolation of phytochemical constituent, characterization and pharmacognostic studies of stem and leaves of *Alangium salvifolium* Wang. The Pharmaceutical and Chemical Journal 2017; 4(5): 89-97.

17) Kasote DM, Katyare SS, Hegde MV, Bae H. Significance of antioxidant potential of plants and its relevance to therapeutic applications. International Journal of Biological Sciences 2015; 11(8): 982-991.

18) Kochuthressia KP. Anti helminthis activity of *Alangium salviifolium* against *Pheretima posthumous*. International Journal of Current Microbiology and Applied Sciences 2018; 7(11): 2720-2724.

19) Marston A, Hostettmann K. Natural product analysis over the last decades. Planta Medica 2009; 75(7): 672-682.

20) Mosaddik MA, Kabir KE, Hassan P. Antibacterial activity of *Alangium salviifolium* flowers. Fitoterapia 2000; 71(4): 447-449.

21) Murugan V, Shareef H, Ramasarma GVS, Ramanathan M, Suresh B. Anti-fertility activity of the stem bark of *Alangium salviifolium* (Linn.F) wang in Wister female rats. Indian Journal of Pharmacology 2000; 32(6): 388-389.

22) Nasrullah M, Haque A, Alzahrani SA, Uddin MA, Yasmin Z, Uddin MS, Almulaiky YQ, Kuerban A. Acetylcholinesterase and butyrylcholinesterase enzyme inhibitory effect of *Alangium salviifolium* (L. f.) Wang pericarp extracts with their phytochemical and antioxidant values. Journal of Pharmaceutical Research International 2017; 19(5): 1-11.

23) Pailee P, Prachyawarakorn V, Ruchirawat S, Mahidol C. Bioactive cardinane sesquiterpenes from the stems of *Alangium salviifolium*. Chemistry An Asian Journal 2015; 10(4): 910-914.

24) Panda SK, Padhi L, Leyssen P, Liu M, Neyts J, Luyten W. Antimicrobial, anthelmintic, and antiviral activity of plants traditionally used for treating infectious disease in the Similipal biosphere reserve, Odisha, India. Frontiers in Pharmacology 2017; 8: 658.

25) Patel AK, Manigauha A. Antioxidant and antidiabetic activity of isolated flavonoids from *Alangium salvifolium* leaves extracts. International Journal of Green Pharmacy 2018; 12(2): 82-90.

26) Prathyusha P. Phytochemical profile and efficacy of free radical scavenging activity of *Alangium salvifolium* (l.f.) Wangerin. International Journal of Science and Research 2018; 7(7): 1028-1032.

27) Rajkumar S, Kumar SN. Isolation chemical characterization and hypoglycemic activity of *Alangium salviifolium* Wang bark in alloxan induced hyperglycemic rats. International Journal of Pharmaceutical Sciences and Research 2011; 2(6): 1518-1524.

28) Ramani AV, Jagajeevanram P. Kalaiselve Extraction and characterization of chromone from *Alangium salvifolium*. Asian Journal of Chemistry 2003; 15(3): 1693-1698.

29) Seca AML, Pinto DCGA. Plant secondary metabolites as anticancer agents: Successes in clinical trials and therapeutic application. International Journal of Molecular Sciences 2018; 19(1): 263.

30) Selin-Rani S, Senthil-Nathan S, Revathi K, Chandrasekaran R, Thanigaivel A, Vasantha-Srinivasan P, Ponsankar A, Edwin ES, Pradeepa V. Toxicity of *Alangium salvifolium* Wang chemical constituents against the tobacco cutworm *Spodoptera litura* Fab. Pesticide Biochemistry and Physiology 2016; 126: 92-101.

31) Sharma AK, Agarwal V, Kumar R, Balasubramaniam A, Mishra A, Gupta R. Pharmacological studies on seeds of *Alangium salvifolium* Linn. Acta Poloniae Pharmaceutica – Drug Research 2011; 68(6): 897-904.

32) Shashikumara S, Prathima C, Sibgatullah M. Evaluation of antidepressant activity of ethanolic extract of *Alangium salviifolium* (L. F.) Wangerin in Swiss albino mice. Biomedical and Pharmacology Journal 2017; 10(1). dx.doi.org/10.13005/bpj/1125.

33) Shravya S, Vinod BN, Sunil C. Pharmacological and phytochemical studies of *Alangium salvifolium* Wang. – A review. Bulletin of Faculty of Pharmacy, Cairo University 2017; 55: 217-222.

34) Tanwer BS, Vijayvergia R. Some biological activities in *Alangium salvifolium* Linn: An endangered plant of India. Journal of Pharmacy Research 2012; 5(5): 2559-2561.

35) Tran MH, Nguyen HD, Kim JC, Choi JS, Lee HK, Min BS. Phenolic glycosides from *Alangium salviifolium* leaves with inhibitory activity on LPS-induced NO, PGE(2), and TNF-alpha production. Bioorganic Medicinal Chemistry Letters 2009; 19(15): 4389-4393.

36) Wolfender JL, Ndjoko K, Hostettmann K. The potential of LC-NMR in phytochemical analysis. Phytochemical Analysis 2001; 12(1): 2-22.

37) Yagi N, Nakahashi H, Kashima Y, Miyazawa M. Isolation and biological activity of a novel cadinane-type sesquiterpenoid from the essential oil of *Alangium salviifolium*. Journal of Oleo Science 2014; 63(12): 1223-1229.

38) Zahan R, Alam BM, Islam SM, Sarker GC, Chowdhury NS, Hosain SB, Mosaddik MA, Jesmin M, Haque EM. Anticancer activity of *Alangium salvifolilum* flower in Ehrlich ascites carcinoma bearing mice. International Journal of Cancer Research 2011; 7(3): 254-262.

39) Zahan R, Mosaddik AM, Barman RK, Wahed MII, Haque EM. Antibacterial and antidiarrhoeal activity of *Alangium salviifolium* Wang flowers. Molecular and Clinical Pharmacology 2012; 2(1): 34-43.

40) Zhou S, Fan F, Sun J, Guo Z, Sun W, Chen L, Tang Q, Qiu G, Yang S, Yu J, Cai Y. Cytotoxic alkaloids from the fruits and seeds of *Alangium salviifolium* (L.f.) Wangerin. Phytochemistry Letters 2018; 26: 195-198.

Cite this chapter as:

Kekuda PTR, Mahalakshmi SN, Chaithra M. Bioactive compounds from *Alangium salviifolium* (L.f.) Wangerin (Cornaceae) – A mini review. In: Kekuda PTR, Vinayaka KS, Raghavendra HL (Editors), Nature and Medicine: Traditional uses, chemistry and bioprospecting of natural products. JPS Scientific Publications, Tamil Nadu, India, 2020, Pp 60 - 72.

Nature and Medicine: Traditional Uses, Chemistry and Bioprocessing of Natural Products
ISBN: 978-81-947154-3-6
First Edition; 2020
Chapter – 7, Page: 73 - 80

7

ELEMENTAL ANALYSIS AND INSECTICIDAL ACTIVITY OF LEAF AND FRUIT OF Alangium salviifolium (L.f.) Wangerin (Cornaceae)

Lavanya D, Soundarya S, Surabhi T. S, Pooja Rao, Prashith Kekuda T. R[*]

Department of Microbiology, S.R.N.M.N College of Applied Sciences, NES Campus, Balraj Urs road, Shivamogga – 577 201, Karnataka, India

*Corresponding author: p.kekuda@gmail.com

Abstract

Alangium salviifolium L. is a medicinally important plant of the family Cornaceae. In this study, we report the mineral content and insecticidal activity of leaf and fruit *A. salviifolium*. The content of nitrogen, potassium, calcium, iron and manganese were found to be present in appreciable quantity in leaf and fruit. Methanolic extract of both leaf and fruit extracts were effective against larvae of *Aedes* species and *Anopheles* species. The present study shows the possible utilization of leaf and fruit of *A. salviifolium* for larval control. The plant, especially the fruit, may be consumed as an important source of various mineral elements.

Key words: *Alangium salviifolium*, Elemental analysis, Maceration, Insecticidal and Larvicidal.

1. Introduction

Unlike carbohydrates, proteins and lipids, mineral elements are required in small quantity and these mineral elements play significant roles such as enzyme cofactors, energy generation, oxygen transport, acid-base balance, nerve transmission, promotion of insulin function and others. Some mineral elements such as calcium, phosphorus, potassium, sodium and magnesium are needed in greater quantity and are designated as macro or major elements whereas minerals such as iron, copper, zinc, manganese, molybdenum and cobalt are required in small quantity and are termed as micro or minor elements. Deficiency or absence of these mineral elements leads to certain disorders. Hence, the diet comprising of these mineral elements in balanced proportion is important for normal health. It is known that various parts of plants such as roots, leaves, and fruits are an integral part of human nutrition. Plants provide important nutrients, vitamins, minerals, antioxidants, dietary fiber, and other phytochemicals that exert profound beneficial effects on human health (Lukaski, 2004; Indrayan *et al.*, 2005; Huskisson *et al.*, 2007; Marles, 2017; Chatepa *et al.*, 2018).

Mosquitoes are considered as public nuisance as they transmit dengue, malaria, yellow fever, chikungunya, filariasis and other diseases leading to considerable morbidity and mortality, especially in developing and under-developing countries. Since many years, management of these mosquito-borne diseases is achieved through the application of synthetic insecticides such as organochlorine and organophosphate compounds. However, their irrational usage of these insecticides results in emergence of resistant races of mosquitoes besides causing serious effects on environment and public health. These drawbacks, together with high cost, associated with the usage of chemicals triggered an upsurge interest in searching alternate strategies to control mosquito vectors. Botanicals are shown to be promising alternatives for synthetic chemicals. Many studies have shown the insecticidal efficacy of crude extracts and purified compounds from plants against mosquitoes (Vinayagam *et al.*, 2008; Vinayaka *et al.*, 2009; Chowdhury *et al.*, 2008; Kim *et al.*, 2017; Mbatchou *et al.*, 2017; Abu Bakar *et al.*, 2018; Achee *et al.*, 2019).

Alangium salviifolium L. belonging to the family Cornaceae is a straggling shrub armed with spines with alternate, broadly elliptic-ovate leaves (up to 15 x 6 cm). The flowers are white, bisexual and borne in axillary fascicles. The fruit is a drupe, ellipsoid, up to 2 cm long, tomentose, purplish-red when ripe and 1-seeded (Bhat, 2014). *A. salviifolium* is widely used in ethnomedicine for treating skin diseases, swellings, scorpion bite, dog bite, bone fracture, tuberculosis, toothache and other ailments or diseases (Survase and Raut, 2011; Pradheeps and Poyyamoli, 2013;

Chapter -7

Raju *et al.*, 2014; Patel and Patel, 2015; Rao, 2015; Kachhi *et al.*, 2018). Experimentally, *A. salviifolium* is shown to display antimicrobial, antioxidant, insecticidal, diuretic, anthelmintic, analgesic, antidiabetic, antifertility, anti-inflammatory, hepatoprotective, and anticancer properties (Jain *et al.*, 2010; Pavunraj *et al.*, 2012; Prakash *et al.*, 2013; Shravya *et al.*, 2017; Patel and Manigauha, 2018). In the present study, we evaluated insecticidal activity and estimated the content of mineral elements in the leaf and fruit of *A. salviifolium*.

2. Materials and Methods

2.1. Collection and identification of plant

A. salviifolium was collected at near Hirejeni, Ripponpet, Shivamogga during December 2018. The plant was identified by Dr. Vinayaka K.S, Assistant Professor and Principal, KFGC, Shikaripura, Karnataka. The leaves and fruits were cleaned, dried under shade and powdered.

2.2. Elemental analysis of leaf and fruit powder

The leaf and fruit powder of *A. salviifolium* were digested using mixture of nitric acid and perchloric acid on hot plate. The digested plant materials were used to estimate the content of major (sodium, potassium, calcium, phosphorus, nitrogen and magnesium) and minor (copper, manganese, iron, zinc, chromium, nickel) elements by various analytical techniques (Swathi *et al.*, 2019).

2.3. Extraction

Maceration technique employing methanol as solvent was used to extract shade dried and powdered leaf and fruit of *A. salviifolium* in separate containers. After 48 hours, filtration was carried out and the filtrates were evaporated to dryness and crude methanolic extract of leaf and fruit were obtained (Raghavendra *et al.*, 2017).

2.4. Insecticidal activity of leaf and fruit extracts

The insecticidal efficacy of leaf and fruit extracts (1 mg extract/ml of water) was determined, in terms of larvicidal effect, against II instar and III instar larvae of *Aedes* species and *Anopheles* species by following the protocol of Vinayaka *et al.* (2009). Larval mortality (%) was determined after 24 hours of exposure of larvae to extracts.

3. Result and Discussion

3.1. Elemental analysis of leaf and fruit of *A. salviifolium*

Literature survey revealed that the leaf and fruit of *A. salviifolium* are edible and consumed by few tribal communities (Yesodharan and Sujana, 2007; Shivprasad *et al.*, 2016; Aadhan and Anand, 2018). In this regard the mineral composition of leaf and fruit extracts of *A. salviifolium* was found out. The content of N and Na were highest and least, respectively, among major elements. Fe and Cr were shown to be in high and least quantity among minor elements. Among major elements, the content of Na, Ca and Mg were highest in leaf while the content of N, P and K were highest in fruit. In case of minor elements, the content of Fe, Mn and Zn were found to be in greater quantity in leaf while Cu, Cr and Ni were detected in highest quantity in fruit (Table - 1).

Table - 1: Mineral content of leaf and fruit of *A. salviifolium*

Mineral	Leaf	Fruit
N (%)	2.27	2.87
Na (%)	0.04	0.03
P (%)	0.125	0.221
K (%)	1.508	1.580
Ca (%)	0.514	0.284
Mg (%)	0.073	0.069
Fe (ppm)	241.65	155.2
Mn (ppm)	48.05	24.65
Zn (ppm)	30.05	28.70
Cu (ppm)	20.85	21.90
Cr (ppm)	3.80	4.95
Ni (ppm)	7.00	7.55

3.2. Insecticidal activity of leaf and fruit extracts

The leaf and fruit extracts of *A. salviifolium* were effective against larvae of both *Aedes* and *Anopheles* mosquitoes. At 1mg/ml extract concentration, a mortality of 100 % was observed in case of II instar larvae of *Anopheles* sp. and II and III instar larvae *Aedes* sp. Leaf extract was shown to produce only 70 % mortality in III instar larvae of *Anopheles* sp. There was no mortality of larvae and pupae in case of DMSO control. (Table - 2 and Figure - 1). In a similar study, Thanigaivel *et al.* (2018) showed insecticidal activity of methanolic extract of *A. salviifolium* leaves against fourth instar larvae of *A. aegypti*. Studies have also shown the insecticidal potential of *A. salviifolium* against *Spodoptera litura* (Pavunraj *et al.*, 2012), *Mythimna separata* (Maheswari *et al.*, 2013), *Sitophilus oryzae* (Prakash *et al.*, 2013), *Culex vishnui* group mosquitoes (Ghosh *et al.*, 2016) and *Culex quinquefasciatus* (Mondal *et al.*, 2016).

Chapter - 7

Table - 2: Insecticidal activity of leaf and fruit extract

Mosquito	Stage	Number of dead larvae out of 20 larvae			
		Leaf extract	Fruit extract	DMSO control	Control (Water)
Anopheles sp.	II instar larvae	20	20	0	0
	III instar larvae	14	20	0	0
Aedes sp.	II instar larvae	20	20	0	0
	III instar larvae	20	20	0	0

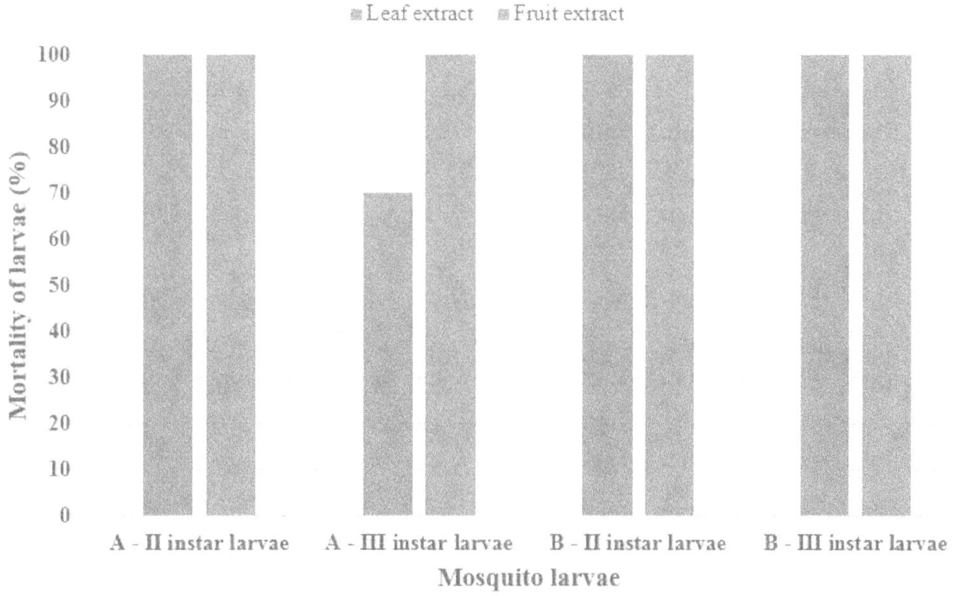

Figure - 1: Mortality of larvae (%) by leaf and fruit extract (A–*Anopheles* species; B–*Aedes* species)

4. Conclusions

Both leaf and fruit of *A. salviifolium* contained major and minor minerals in good quantity highlighting the potential utilization of the plant for edible purpose. Marked susceptibility of larvae of *Aedes* species and *Anopheles* species to leaf and fruit extracts highlights the possible utilization of the plant for managing the mosquito vectors and mosquito-borne diseases.

Acknowledgements

Authors thank Head, Dept. of Microbiology and Principal, S.R.N.M.N College of Applied Sciences for providing facilities to conduct the work. Authors thank Dr. Vinayaka K.S, Principal, K.F.G.C, Shikaripura for helping in collection and identification of the plant. Authors also thank Ms. Mahalakshmi S.N., Lecturer,

Department of Zoology, S.R.N.M.N College of Applied Sciences, Shivamogga for helping in identification of larvae.

5. References

1) Aadhan K, Anand SP. Utilization of wild edible plants by Paliyar's tribe of Sadhuragiri hills, Tamil Nadu, India. International Journal of Recent Scientific Research 2018; 9(5): 27090-27096.

2) Abu Bakar A, Sulaiman S, Omar B, Ali RM. Screening of five plant extracts for larvicidal efficacy against larvae of *Aedes aegypti* (L.) and *Aedes albopictus* (Skuse). ASM Sci J. 2018; 11(2): 103-116.

3) Achee NL, Grieco JP, Vatandoost H, Seixas G, Pinto J, Ching-NG L, Martins AJ, Juntarajumnong W, Corbel V, Gouagna C, David J, Logan JG, Orsborne J, Marois E, Devine GJ, Vontas J. Alternative strategies for mosquito-borne arbovirus control. PLoS Negl Trop Dis. 2019; 13(1): e0006822.

4) Bhat GK. Flora of South Kanara. Akriti Prints, Mangalore, India, 2014.

5) Chatepa LEC, Masamba K, Jose M. Proximate composition, physical characteristics and mineral content of fruit, pulp and seeds of *Parinari curatellifolia* (Maula) from Central Malawi. Afr J Food Sci. 2018; 12(9): 238-245.

6) Chowdhury N, Laskar S, Chandra G. Mosquito larvicidal and antimicrobial activity of protein of *Solanum villosum* leaves. BMC Complementary Altern Med. 2008; 8: 62.

7) Ghosh P, Mondal RP, Haldar KM, Chandra G. Larvicidal, pupicidal and smoke toxic activity of *Alangium salviifolium* leaf extracts against *Culex vishnui* group mosquitoes. Journal of Mosquito Research 2016; 6(2): 1-8.

8) Huskisson E, Maggini S, Ruf M. The role of vitamins and minerals in energy metabolism and well-being. J Int Med Res. 2007; 35: 277.

9) Indrayan AK, Sharma S, Durgapal D, Kumar N, Kumar M. Determination of nutritive value and analysis of mineral elements for some medicinally valued plants from Uttaranchal. Curr Sci. 2005; 89(7): 1252-1255.

10) Jain VC, Patel NM, Shah DP, Patel KP, Joshi BH. Antioxidant and antimicrobial activities of *Alangium salviifolium* (leaf) Wang root. Global J Pharmacol. 2010; 4(1): 13-18.

11) Kachhi RS, Saket VK, Sharma P, Singh P. Treatment of tuberculosis using ethno-medicinal plants of Amarkantak region. Asian J Anim Vet Adv. 2018; 13(1): 52-60.

12) Kim S, Ahn Y. Larvicidal activity of lignans and alkaloid identified in *Zanthoxylum piperitum* bark toward insecticide-susceptible and wild *Culex pipiens pallens* and *Aedes aegypti*. Parasites Vectors 2017; 10: 221.

13) Lukaski HC. Vitamin and mineral status: Effects on physical performance. Nutrition 2004; 20(7/8): 632-644.

14) Maheswari S, Chitra M, Sivasangari R. Isolation of insecticidal compound from *Alangium salviifolium* and its effect on *Mythimna separata*. Research Journal of Agriculture and Environmental Management 2013; 2(8): 229-232.

15) Marles RJ. Mineral nutrient composition of vegetables, fruits and grains: The context of reports of apparent historical declines. J Food Comp Anal. 2017; 56: 93-103.

16) Mbatchou VC, Tchouassi DP, Dickson RA, Annan K, Mensah AY, Amponsah IK, Jacob JW, Cheseto X, Habtemariam S, Torto B. Mosquito larvicidal activity of *Cassia tora* seed extract and its key anthraquinones aurantio-obtusin and obtusin. Parasites Vectors 2017; 10: 562.

17) Mondal RP, Singh A, Ghosh A, Chandra G. Studies on larvicidal activity of some plant extracts against filarial vector *Culex quinquefasciatus.* Journal of Mosquito Research 2016; 6(7): 1-6.

18) Patel AK, Manigauha A. Antioxidant and antidiabetic activity of isolated flavonoids from *Alangium salviifolium* leaves extracts. Int J Green Pharm. 2018; 12(2): 82-90.

19) Patel NB, Patel KB. Ethnomedicinal plants used by the tribals of district Sabarkantha, Gujarat, India. J Med Plants Stud. 2015; 4(3): 179-181.

20) Pavunraj M, Pulraj GM, Kumar SS, Rao MRK, Ignacimuthu S. Feeding deterrence, larvicidal and haemolymph protein profiles of an Indian traditional medicinal plant *Alangium salviifolium* (L.F.) Wangerin on cluster caterpillar, *Spodoptera litura* (Fabricius) (Lepidoptera: Noctuidae). Arch Phytopathol Plant Protect. 2012; 45(17): 2066-2075.

21) Pradheeps M, Poyyamoli G. Ethnobotany and utilization of plant resources in Irula villages (Sigur plateau, Nilgiri Biosphere Reserve, India). J Med Plants Res. 2013; 7(6): 267-276.

22) Prakash UNK, Bhuvaneswari S, Preethy S, Rajalakshmi N, Saranya M, Anto JR, Arokiyaraj S. Studies on antimicrobial, antioxidant, larvicidal, pesticidal activity and phytochemistry of leaves of *Alangium salviifolium* (L.f) Wang. Int J Pharm Pharm Sci. 2013; 5(2): 86-89.

23) Raghavendra HL, Kekuda PTR, Akarsh S, Ranjitha MC, Ashwini HS. Phytochemical analysis, antimicrobial and antioxidant activities of different parts of *Pleocaulus sessilis* (Nees) Bremek (Acanthaceae). Int J Green Pharm. 2017; 11(2): 98-107.

24) Raju RY, Yugandhar P, Savithramma N. Documentation of ethnomedicinal knowledge of hilly tract areas of East Godavri District of Andhra Pradesh, India. Int J Pharm Pharm Sci. 2014; 6(4): 369-374.

25) Rao SS. Ethno botanical study of medicinal plants of Sri Pancha Narasimha Swamy and Sri Matsyagiri Narasimha Swamy. J Med Plants Stud. 2015; 3(3): 37-42.

26) Shivprasad M, Rane M, Manik P. Traditional uses of some wild edible fruits from Palghar district. J Nat Prod Plant Resour. 2016; 6(6): 8-11.

27) Shravya S, Vinod BN, Sunil C. Pharmacological and phytochemical studies of *Alangium salviifolium* Wang. – A review. Bull Fac Pharm Cairo Univ. 2017; 55(2): 217-222.

28) Swathi BG, Smruthi BS, Banu S, Kekuda PTR. Insecticidal, antimicrobial and antioxidant activity and elemental analysis of *Cochlospermum religiosum* (L.) Alston (Bixaceae). Journal of Drug Delivery and Therapeutics 2019; 9(2S): 422-428.

29) Thanigaivel A, Vasantha-Srinivasan P, Edwin ES, Ponsankar A, Selin-Rani S, Chellapandian M, Kelaivani K, Senthil-Nathan S, Benelli G. Development of an eco-friendly mosquitocidal agent from *Alangium salviifolium* against the dengue vector *Aedes aegypti* and its biosafety on the aquatic predator. Environ Sci Pollut Res. 2018; 25 (11): 10340-10352.

30) Vinayagam A, Senthilkumar N, Umamaheswari A. Larvicidal activity of some medicinal plant extracts against malaria vector *Anopheles stephensi*. Research Journal of Parasitology 2008; 3(2): 50-58.

31) Vinayaka KS, Kumar SVP, Kekuda PTR, Krishnamurthy YL, Mallikarjun N, Swathi D. Proximate composition, antioxidant, anthelmintic and insecticidal activity of a macrolichen *Ramalina conduplicans* Vain. (Ramalinaceae). European Journal of Applied Sciences 2009; 1(3): 40-46.

32) Yesodharan K, Sujana KA. Wild edible plants traditionally used by the tribes in the Parambikulam wildlife sanctuary, Kerala, India. Natural Product Radiance 2007; 6(1): 74-80.

Cite this chapter as:

Lavanya D, Soundarya S, Surabhi TS, Rao P, Kekuda PTR. Elemental analysis and insecticidal activity of leaf and fruit of *Alangium salviifolium* (L.f.) Wangerin (Cornaceae). In: Kekuda PTR, Vinayaka KS, Raghavendra HL (Editors), Nature and Medicine: Traditional uses, chemistry and bioprospecting of natural products. JPS Scientific Publications, Tamil Nadu, India, 2020, Pp 73 - 80.

Nature and Medicine: Traditional Uses, Chemistry and Bioprocessing of Natural Products
ISBN: 978-81-947154-3-6
First Edition; 2020
Chapter – 8, Page: 81 - 87

8

In vitro ANTIFUNGAL AND ANTIRADICAL ACTIVITY OF GRAPE SEED EXTRACT

Nandini V, Shreya K. S, Fathima Mohammadi, Prashith Kekuda T. R[*]

Department of Microbiology, S.R.N.M.N College of Applied Sciences, NES Campus, Balraj Urs road,
Shivamogga – 577 201, Karnataka, India
*Corresponding author: p.kekuda@gmail.com

Abstract

Grape seed extract (GSE) obtained by maceration process was screened for antifungal and antiradical activity *in vitro*. The GSE was effective against two seed-borne *Aspergillus* species *viz. A. niger* and *A. flavus* with marked activity against *A. niger* (44.4 % inhibition) when compared to *A. flavus* (35.8 % inhibition). The GSE was shown to scavenge DPPH radicals dose dependently with an IC_{50} value of 13.72 µg/ml. GSE is a promising alternative for developing formulations for managing oxidative damage and seed-borne fungi

Key words: Grape, Maceration, seed-borne fungi, Poisoned food technique and DPPH.

1. Introduction

Seeds are the main input for production of several crops. Many Seeds of agricultural and horticultural crops are associated with several mold species such as species of *Aspergillus*, *Penicillium*, *Mucor*, *Rhizoctonia*, *Rhizopus*, *Alternaria*, *Curvuralia*, *Macrophomina*, *Fusarium*, and *Bipolaris*. Fungi represents dominant group of plant pathogens that are transmitted through seeds. Many of these fungi are known to deteriorate seed quality and often reduce seedling vigor. Management of phytopathogenic fungi including seed-borne fungi is achieved by the application of

synthetic fungicides, however, their indiscriminate use leads to environmental pollution, toxic effects of human health and development of resistance in fungi. There is constant search for alternatives for the management of plant pathogenic fungi and botanicals are considered to be one of the fruitful alternatives for the management of seed-borne fungi (Thobunluepop, 2009; Panchal and Dhale, 2011; Yago *et al.*, 2011; Ghangaokar and Kshirsagar, 2013; Yoon *et al.*, 2013; Shuping and Eloff, 2017; Moumni *et al.*, 2020).

A small amount of oxygen that is inhaled is converted into reactive oxygen species (ROS) such as free radicals (superoxide radical and hydroxyl radical) and non-radical species (hydrogen peroxide and singlet oxygen) are formed in the cells during normal metabolism as well as on exposure to certain environmental conditions. These ROS are known to induce oxidative stress triggering conditions such as cancer, cardiovascular diseases, neurodegenerative diseases and ageing. Antioxidants are the substances that mitigate the toxic effect of these ROS. Antioxidant defense system of the cell include enzymes namely superoxide dismutase and catalase and small molecules such as vitamin C, vitamin E and glutatione. It is shown that polyphenolic compounds (including flavonoids) represents the dominant group of phytochemicals that exert potential antioxidant activity. Plants and their metabolites are shown to be significant with respect to protection of the body against toxic ROS (Gupta and Sharma, 2006; Krishnaiah *et al.*, 2011; Junaid *et al.*, 2013; Xu *et al.*, 2017; Stagos, 2020).

Grapes (*Vitis vinifera* L.) represents one of the most important fruit crops grown worldwide with about 80 % of the harvest being used for wine making. The pomace i.e. the solid grape residues that consists of skin and seeds are the waste byproducts that is generated in huge quantities by the winemaking industries. The seeds of grapes represents around 15 % of the solid waste. It is shown that the grape seeds are well-known dietary supplement as they contain minerals, vitamins, and polyphenols. Catechins, epicatechin, and procyanidin are the abundant phenolic compounds present in grape seeds and these polyphenols are recognized for health promoting role. The grape seeds are shown to display pharmacological activities such as antioxidant, anti-inflammatory, antimicrobial, anticancer, antiviral, cardioprotective, hepatoprotective, neuroprotective, anti-ageing and antidiabetic activities. The oil extracted from grape seeds finds several applications such as cosmetic, culinary, and medical purposes (Baydar *et al.*, 2007; Li *et al.*, 2008; Suwannaphet *et al.*, 2010; Canbay and Bardakçı, 2011; Su and D'Souza, 2011; Mendes *et al.*, 2013; Ranjitha *et al.*, 2014; Gupta *et al.*, 2020; Ao and Kim, 2020). The

present study evaluates antifungal and antiradical potential of methanolic extract of grape seeds.

2. Materials and Methods

2.1. Preparation of grape seed extract (GSE)

The grape seeds were cleaned and powdered. A known quantity of seed powder was subjected to extraction by maceration process and methanol was used as menstruum (Raghavendra *et al.*, 2017).

2.2. Antifungal activity of GSE

Antifungal activity of GSE (1mg extract/ml of potato dextrose agar) was tested against *Aspergillus niger* and *A. flavus* by poisoned food technique as described in the study of Raghavendra *et al.* (2017). The growth of test fungi in poisoned plates was measured (colony diameter) and compared with fungal growth in control plates (without extract).

2.3. Antiradical activity of GSE

The potential of different concentrations of GSE (3.12 to 50 µg/ml) to exhibit antiradical activity was assessed by 2,2-diphenyl-1-picryl hydrazyl (DPPH) assay as described in the study of Raghavendra *et al.* (2017). Ascorbic acid was used as reference standard. IC_{50} value was calculated.

3. Results and Discussion

3.1. Antifungal activity of GSE

The GSE was subjected to antifungal activity by poisoned food technique which is one among various *in vitro* techniques available to investigate antifungal nature of botanicals. A decrease in the colony size of the fungus in poisoned plates indicates antifungal potential of a sample or substance (Kambar *et al.*, 2014; Pushpavathi *et al.*, 2017). The GSE was shown to display inhibitory activity against both the fungi. Considerable reduction in the mycelial growth as well as sporulation of test fungi was observed in poisoned plates (Table - 1). Among fungi, marked susceptibility to GSE was shown by *A. niger* (44.4 % inhibition) when compared to *A. flavus* (35.8 % inhibition). In a previous study by Ranjitha *et al.* (2014), the GSE was shown to display mycelial growth inhibition of *Colletotrichum capsici*.

Table 1: Antifungal activity of GSE

Treatment	Colony diameter in cm	
	Control	% inhibition
Control	4.5	2.5
GSE	3.9	2.5

3.2. Antiradical activity of GSE

The method that involves scavenging of stable, organic and nitrogen centred DPPH radical is widely used to screen antiradical activity of plant extracts. In this assay, the substances (i.e. antioxidants) that have the potential to donate proton will convert DPPH radicals (purple color) into DPPHH (diphenylpicryl hydrazine, yellow color). This method has been extensively used to screen antiradical potential of several botanicals by researchers (Junaid *et al.*, 2013; Raghavendra *et al.*, 2017; Youn *et al.*, 2018; Costa *et al.*, 2019). In our study, the GSE was shown to exhibit concentration dependent scavenging of DPPH radicals and a scavenging activity of 50 % and higher was observed at extract concentration 12.50 µg/ml and higher (Figure - 1). Ascorbic acid scavenged DPPH radicals dose dependently and more efficiently with an IC_{50} value of 6.89 µg/ml when compared to GSE (IC_{50} value 13.72 µg/ml). Earlier studies by Katsuda *et al.* (2015), Costa *et al.* (2019), and Gleńsk *et al.* (2019) also reported scavenging potential of GSE/compounds isolated from GSE against DPPH radicals.

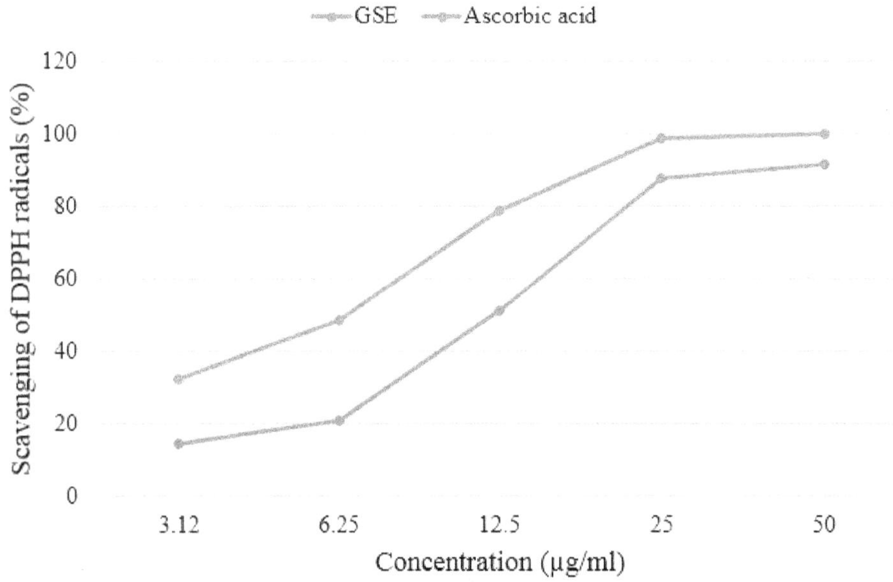

Figure - 1: Scavenging of DPPH radicals by GSE

4. Conclusions

The GSE exhibited antifungal and antiradical potential. GSE seems to be a promising candidate for developing antimycotic and antiradical agents or formulations. Recovery of active principles from the extract and their antifungal and antiradical activity determinations are merited in further studies.

Acknowledgements

Authors thank Head, Department of Microbiology and the Principal, S.R.N.M.N College of Applied Sciences, Shivamogga and the Management, N.E.S, Shivamogga for providing facilities to conduct work.

5. References

1) Ao X, Kim IH. Effects of grape seed extract on performance, immunity, antioxidant capacity, and meat quality in Pekin ducks. Poultry Science 2020r; 99(4): 2078-2086.

2) Baydar NG, Özkan G, Çetin ES. Characterization of grape seed and pomace oil extracts. Grasas Y Aceites 2007; 58(1): 29-33.

3) Canbay HS, Bardakçı B. Determination of fatty acid, C, H, N and trace element composition in grape seed by GC/MS, FTIR, elemental analyzer and ICP/OES. SDU Journal of Science (E-Journal) 2011; 6(2): 140-148.

4) Costa GN, Tonon RV, Mellinger-Silva C, Galdeano MC, Iacomini M, Santiago MC, Almeida EL, Freitas SP. Grape seed pomace as a valuable source of antioxidant fibers. Journal of the Science of Food and Agriculture 2019; 99(10): 4593-4601.

5) Geta K. Efficiency of medicinal plants to control seed borne fungi of sorghum grains. SOJ Microbiology and Infectious Diseases 2019; 7(2): 1-3.

6) Ghangaokar NM, Kshirsagar AD. Study of seed borne fungi of different legumes. Trends in Life Sciences 2013; 2(1): 32-35.

7) Gleńsk M, Hurst WJ, Glinski VB, Bednarski M, Gliński JA. Isolation of 1-(3',4'-Dihydroxyphenyl)-3-(2″,4″,6″-trihydroxyphenyl)-propan-2-ol from grape seed extract and evaluation of its antioxidant and antispasmodic potential. Molecules 2019; 24(13): 2466.

8) Gupta M, Dey S, Marbaniang D, Pal P, Ray S, Mazumder B. Grape seed extract: having a potential health benefits. Journal of Food Science and Technology 2020; 57(4): 1205-1215.

9) Gupta VK, Sharma SK. Plants as natural antioxidants. Natural Product Radiance 2006; 5(4): 326-334.

10) Junaid S, Rakesh KN, Dileep N, Poornima G, Kekuda PTR, Mukunda S. Total phenolic content and antioxidant activity of seed extract of *Lagerstroemia speciosa* L. Chemical Science Transactions 2013; 2(1): 75-80.

11) Kambar Y, Manasa M, Vivek MN, Kekuda PTR. Inhibitory effect of some plants of Western Ghats of Karnataka against *Colletotrichum capsici*. Science, Technology Arts Research Journal 2014; 3(2): 76-82.

12) Katsuda Y, Niwano Y, Nakashima T, Mokudai T, Nakamura K, Oizumi S, Kanno T, Kanetaka H, Egusa H. Cytoprotective effects of grape seed extract on human gingival fibroblasts in relation to its antioxidant potential. PLoS One 2015; 10(8): e0134704.

13) Krishnaiah D, Sarbatly R, Nithyanandam R. A review of the antioxidant potential of medicinal plant species. Food and Bioproducts Processing 2011; 89(3): 217-233.

14) Li H, Wang X, Li P, Li Y, Wang H. Comparative study of antioxidant activity of grape (*Vitis vinifera*) seed powder assessed by different methods. Journal of Food and Drug Analysis 2008; 16(6): 1-7.

15) Mendes JAS, Prozil SO, Evtuguin DV, Lopes LPC. Towards comprehensive utilization of winemaking residues: Characterization of grape skins from red grape pomaces of variety Touriga Nacional. Industrial Crops and Products 2013; 43: 25-32.

16) Moumni M, Allagui MB, Mancini V, Murolo S, Tarchoun N, Romanazzi G. Morphological and molecular identification of seedborne Fungi in Squash (*Cucurbita maxima, Cucurbita moschata*). Plant Disease 2020; 104(5): 1335-1350.

17) Panchal VH, Dhale DA. Isolation of seed-borne fungi of sorghum (*Sorghum vulgare* pers.). Journal of Phytology 2011; 3(12): 45-48.

18) Pushpavathi D, Shilpa M, Petkar T, Siddiqha A, Kekuda PTR. Evaluation of antifungal activity of some plants against seed-borne fungi. Scholars Journal of Agriculture and Veterinary Sciences 2017; 4(4): 155-159.

19) Raghavendra HL, Kekuda PTR, Pushpavathi D, Shilpa M, Petkar T, Siddiqha A. Antimicrobial, radical scavenging, and insecticidal activity of leaf and flower extracts of *Couroupita guianensis* Aubl. International Journal of Green Pharmacy 2017; 11(3): 171-179.

20) Ranjitha CY, Priyanka S, Deepika R, Smitha Rani GP, Sahana J, Kekuda PTR. Antimicrobial activity of grape seed extract. World Journal of Pharmacy and Pharmaceutical Sciences 2014; 3(8): 1483-1488.

21) Shuping DSS, Eloff JN. The use of plants to protect plants and food against fungal pathogens: A review. African Journal of Traditional, Complementary Alternative Medicine 2017; 14(4): 120-127.

22) Stagos D. Antioxidant activity of polyphenolic plant extracts. Antioxidants 2020; 9: 19.

23) Su X, D'Souza DH. Grape seed extract for control of human enteric viruses. Applied and Environmental Microbiology 2011; 77(12): 3982-3987.

24) Suwannaphet W, Meeprom A, Yibchok-Anun S, Adisakwattana S. Preventive effect of grape seed extract against high-fructose diet-induced insulin resistance and oxidative stress in rats. Food and Chemical Toxicology 2010; 48: 1853–1857.

25) Thobunluepop P. Implementation of Bio-Fungicides and Seed Treatment in Organic Rice cv. KDML 105 Farming. Pakistan Journal of Biological Sciences 2009; 12: 1119-1126.

26) Xu DP, Li Y, Meng X, Zhou T, Zhou Y, Zheng J, Zhang JJ, Li HB. Natural Antioxidants in Foods and Medicinal Plants: Extraction, Assessment and Resources. International Journal of Molecular Sciences 2017; 18(1): 96.

27) Yago JI, Roh JH, Bae SD, Yoon YN, Kim HJ, Nam MH. The Effect of Seed-borne Mycoflora from Sorghum and Foxtail Millet Seeds on Germination and Disease Transmission. Mycobiology 2011; 39(3): 206-218.

28) Yoon MY, Cha B, Kim JC. Recent trends in studies on botanical fungicides in agriculture. Plant Pathology Journal 2013; 29(1): 1-9.

29) Youn JS, Kim YJ, Na HJ, Jung HR, Song CK, Kang SY, Kim JY. Antioxidant activity and contents of leaf extracts obtained from *Dendropanax morbifera* LEV are dependent on the collecting season and extraction conditions. Food Science and Biotechnology 2018; 28(1): 201-207.

Nature and Medicine: Traditional Uses, Chemistry and Bioprocessing of Natural Products
ISBN: 978-81-947154-3-6
First Edition; 2020
Chapter – 9, Page: 88 - 100

9

ETHNOVETERINARY POTENTIAL OF *Vitex negundo* L. (Lamiaceae) – A REVIEW

Prashith Kekuda T. R[1] and Mahalakshmi S. N[2*]

[1]Department of Microbiology, S.R.N.M.N College of Applied Sciences, NES Campus, Balraj Urs road,
Shivamogga – 577 201, Karnataka, India
[2]Department of Zoology, S.R.N.M.N College of Applied Sciences, NES Campus, Balraj Urs road,
Shivamogga – 577 201, Karnataka, India

*Corresponding author: mahalakshmisn94@gmail.com

Abstract

Domesticated animals play a significant role in human civilization and the rearing animals for various needs such as meat, milk, hide, manure, agricultural practices and other needs has been recorded since time immemorial. Plants have been considered as an important component of ethnoveterinary medicine and many plant species have been widely used all over the world to treat several diseases of animals. In this review, we report various ethnoveterinary applications whole plant and different parts of *Vitex negundo* L. (Lamiaceae). Information was collected from journals, Google and other search engines such as Google Scholar, PubMed and ScienceDirect. The plant is reported to be one of the widely used ethnoveterinary plants in India and other countries such as Nepal, Pakistan and Bangladesh. Several tribal communities across India and other parts of the world exploit different parts of *V. negundo* for the treatment of veterinary ailments. The plant is used in the treatment of diseases or conditions such as mastitis, foot and mouth disease, eye infection, fracture, worm infestation, wound, anthrax, fever, infectious disease, snake bite, dermatitis, bloating, arthritis, breathing problem, diarrhea and dysentery. The plant, especially leaves, has also been used to eradicate ectoparasites. *V. negundo* can be

studied for phytochemical agents with activity against veterinary ailments and future studies may be undertaken as a way for developing new drugs from this plant for veterinary diseases.

Key words: *Vitex negundo*, Traditional medicine and Ethnoveterinary.

1. Introduction

The daily life of humans and other animals depend on plants in one or the other way as plants are important resources of food, medicine and fodder. Plants have been a key component of traditional medicine being used to treat various diseases or disorders of humans as well as animals. Plant based medicines are popular in developing and under-developing countries. However, herbal medicine is gaining popularity in developed countries nowadays. People living in villages or remote places prefer to adapt herbal medicine because of low cost, no or negligible side effects and easy availability. Plants have been considered as treasure sources of several bioactive secondary metabolites such as morphine, vincristine and vinblastine possessing novel therapeutic applications (Ganesan *et al.*, 2007-2008; Poornima *et al.*, 2012; Mishra *et al.*, 2015; Seyoum *et al.*, 2015; Baidya *et al.*, 2020; Singh *et al.*, 2020; Nimbalkar *et al.*, 2020).

2. Ethnoveterinary uses of plants

Since time immemorial, humans have domesticated and used several animal species for various needs such as meat, milk, hide, manure and for agricultural practices. Domesticated animals and birds have been one of the important sources of income for several indigenous and rural communities. However, rearing and breeding of various animals/birds such as cow, buffalo, goat, sheep and chicken is often challenged by various diseases or ailments. Diseases such as foot and mouth disease, mastitis, anthrax, worm infestation and avian influenza pose serious threat to animal husbandry resulting in considerable economic loss. In order to treat diseases or sickness of animals, a wide range of plants have been used either singly or in certain polyherbal formulations. Plants have been extensively used in ethnoveterinary medicine by several tribal communities all over the world. Herbal medicaments are promising with respect to their efficacy in controlling several animal illnesses (Bhatt *et al.*, 2013; Saha *et al.*, 2014; Mishra *et al.*, 2015; Panda and Mishra, 2016; Pushpangadan *et al.*, 2016; Ranganathan, 2017; Sikarwar and Tiwari, 2020).

Chapter - 9

3. *Vitex negundo* L. (Lamiaceae)

V. negundo (Figure - 1) is a large shrub or a small tree with leaves 3-5 foliolate. The plant is common in waste lands and hedges. It is commonly known as Chinese chaste tree, five-leaved chaste tree in English, Nirgundi in Sanskrit, Notchi in Tamil and Lakki gida in Kannada. The leaves are glabrous above and whitish or purple tomentose beneath. Panicles terminal, up to 30cm long, sometimes also form upper axils. Corolla is bluish purple and approximately 1 cm long. Fruit is a drupe, globular, up to 0.5 cm wide and becomes black on ripening. Flowering may occur more or less throughout year (Bhat, 2014; Ahuja *et al.*, 2015). Roots and leaves of the plant are widely used as medicine. *V. negundo* has several ritual uses. The plant has been extensively used in ethnomedicine for treating human and veterinary ailments. Many bioactive phytochemicals have been identified in *V. negundo*. It has been shown that *V. negundo* exhibit pharmacological activities such as anticonvulsant, antioxidant, insecticidal, anti-inflammatory, hypoglycemic, hepatoprotective, antitumor, and analgesic activities (Dharmasiri *et al.*, 2003; Tendon, 2005; Prakasha and Krishnappa, 2006; Kamruzzaman *et al.*, 2013; Bhat, 2014; Zheng *et al.*, 2015; Ahuja *et al.*, 2015). In this review, we have discussed ethnoveterinary uses of *V. negundo* with special reference to its traditional utilization in India.

Figure - 1: *V. negundo* (Photograph by Kavya Shastri)

4. Ethnoveterinary applications of *V. negundo* in India

Different parts of *V. negundo* are used either singly or in some formulations in the form of decoction, paste, poultice etc. to treat various veterinary ailments in India. In Nimar region, Madhya Pradesh, the plant is used in placenta retention in cattle (Preeti, 2018). In Villupuram district, Tamil Nadu, the decoction prepared from leaves is used to cure body pain and cough in cattle. The smoke from leaves is

used to get rid of ectoparasites (Dhanam and Elayaraj, 2014). In Perambalur district, Tamil Nadu, the plant is used to treat ephemeral fever and anthrax (Devendrakumar and Anbazhagan, 2012). The Lambani community in Chitradurga district, Karnataka, uses the roots, leaves and bark of *V. negundo* to treat diarrhea (Naik *et al.*, 2012). In Shivpuri district of Madhya Pradesh, the leaves of *V. negundo* are used to cure infectious diseases in cows (Jatav *et al.*, 2014). In Pratapgarh district of Rajasthan, the leaves are used to treat stomachache (Meena, 2014). The Malayali tribe of Kalrayan (Kalvarayan) hills, Eastern Ghats of the Southern Indian state of Tamil Nadu use leaves for treating udder infection (Kannan *et al.*, 2016). In Rajasthan, *V. negundo* is used to treat high fever in camel (Meena *et al.*, 2020). In Jajpur district of Orissa, the leaves are used to treat cuts, wounds, breathing trouble and flatulence (Satapathy, 2010).

In Akola district, Maharashtra, the leaves of *V. negundo* are used to treat diarrhea in cattle (Dhore and Undal, 2017). In Ganjam district, Odisha, the paste made from the leaves is employed to treat breathing trouble (Adhikary, 2014). The gandigawad tribe of Khanapur taluka of Belgaum district, Karnataka utilize tender leaves to treat infectious diseases and the leaf paste in bone fracture (Holennavar and Kulkarni, 2015). In Bareilly district, Uttar Pradesh, the leaves and roots of *V. negundo* are used for treating wounds in goats (Sasikala *et al.*, 2018). The juice prepared from leaves is used to cure rheumatism in Kalahandi district, Orissa (Sadangi and Sahu, 2004). The tribals of north - east Chhattisgarh uses stem bark to manage dysentery in cow and buffalo (Ekka, 2015). The tribal community of Chittoor district, Andhra Pradesh employ the plant for deworming (intestinal worms) and treatment of pneumonia (Jagadeeswary *et al.*, 2014). The juice made from the roots is administered orally to treat mastitis in Sariska region, Rajasthan (Upadhyay *et al.*, 2011). In Adilabad district, Andhra Pradesh, the leaf extract is sprayed over animals for eradication of lice (Ramana, 2008). The tribals of Birbhum district, West Bengal utilize leaves to treat bone fracture (Rahaman *et al.*, 2009).

The tribal communities of Koraput, Odisha, the leaf paste is given orally to cow to manage stomach infection (Lenka *et al.*, 2018). The fumes from dried leaves are used to repel mosquitoes by Birhore tribes of Jharkhand (Mairh and Mishra, 2015). The leaf juice is put in the nostril of cattle for treating poisonous bites (Sreenivasa and Kumar, 2017). In Kovilpatti taluk, Tuticorin district of Tamil Nadu, the paste made from leaves is used to treat swellings (Siva *et al.*, 2016). The residents of mahal village of dang district, Gujarat utilize the leaves to relieve muscle and joint pain (Gayakvad *et al.*, 2014). In Rajouri (J&K), the leaf decoction is used to treat cough and body pain in cattle (Jamwal and Kant, 2008). Jende Kuruba community

in Athani taluka, Belgaum district of Karnataka use the leaves to treat fever and fracture (Emmi, 2015). In Erode district, Tamil Nadu, the smoke from leaves is used to eradicate ectoparasites in poultry (Vinothraj *et al.*, 2019). In southern districts of Tamil Nadu, leaves of the plant are used for bronchitis and corneal opaceity (Ganesan *et al.*, 2008). In Sringeri taluk, Karnataka, the leaf extract is used to treat limb pain, cracks, swellings and wounds in cattle (Prakasha and Krishnappa, 2006). More information on ethnoveterinary uses of different parts of *V. negundo* in India is presented in Table 1.

Table 1: Ethnoveterinary uses of V. negundo in India

Area	Part used	Uses	References
Nimar region, Madhya Pradesh, India	Root (paste)	Mastitis	Preeti and Solanki (2016)
Honnavar, Karnataka	Leaf	Bone displacement	Guruprasad and Prasad (2019)
Central India	Leaf (paste)	Wounds	Sikarwar and Kumar (2005)
Bhandara district (M.S.) India	Leaf	Muscular pain, infectious diseases	Gadpayale *et al.* (2014)
Tirupur district, Tamil Nadu, India	Leaf (paste)	Bronchitis	Selvi *et al.* (2015)
Himachal Pradesh, India	Leaf, bark, flowers	Cough, skin infection, sprain, food and mouth disease	Radha *et al.* (2020)
Tamil Nadu, India	Leaf (paste)	Diarrhea, foot and mouth disease, fever, flu	Jayakumar *et al.* (2018)
Cape Comorin, India	Leaf	Worm problem	Kiruba *et al.* (2006)
Namakkal district, Tamil Nadu, India	Leaf	Snake bite, antibacterial	Bhuvaneswari *et al.* (2015)
Udupi district, Karnataka, India	Leaf	Worm infestation in animal hooves	Dhananjaya *et al.* (2018)
Marwar region, Rajasthan, India	Stem (decoction)	Mange, fever	Meen *et al.* (2020)
Betul district, Madhya Pradesh, India	Leaf	Swelling, fracture, snake bite	Deshmukh and Pochhi (2011)
Akola district, Maharashtra, India	Leaf (juice)	Eye diseases	Jambu and Wath (2018)
Himachal Pradesh, India	Leaf	Bloating, fever, mastitis	Saini and Sood (2018)
Thiruvarur district, Tamil Nadu, India	Leaf, root	Infectious diseases, diarrhea, dysentery	Parthiban *et al.* (2016)
Tikamgarh district, Bundelkhand	Leaf	Diarrhea	Verma (2014)
Wardha district, Maharashtra	Leaf	Galse	Pranjale & Dube (2016)
Madhya Pradesh, India	Leaf	Cut and injury	Sumeet *et al.* (2009)
Visakhapatnam, Andhra Pradesh, India	Leaf	Wound, anthrax	Narayana and Narasimharao (2015)
Junagah, Gujarat	Leaf	Mild to moderate inflammation	Bhatt *et al.* (2019)
Uttara Kannada district, Karnataka	Leaf	Poisonous bite	Harsha *et al.* (2005)

Chapter - 9

Tadgarh-Raoli wildlife sanctuary, Rajasthan	Leaf	Food and mouth disease, ephemeral fever	Galav *et al.* (2013)
Salem district, Tamil Nadu	Leaf	Breathing problem	Alagesaboopathi (2015)
Koch Bihar district, West Bengal	Leaf, root	Leaf in pain due to sprain, root in mastitis	Bandyopadhyay and Mukherjee (2005)
Odisha, India	Leaf	Breathing problem	Mallik *et al.* (2012)
Kathua, Jammu and Kashmir	Leaf	Eye infection	Sharma *et al.* (2012)
Senapathi district, Manipur	-	Dermatitis	Rajkumari *et al.* (2014)

5. Ethnoveterinary applications of *V. negundo* in other countries

V. negundo is also used as one of the ethnoveterinary plants in other countries such as Bangladesh, Pakistan, and Nepal. A brief description of ethnoveterinary uses of *V. negundo* is presented in Table - 2.

Table - 2: *V. negundo* as an ethnoveterinary plant in other countries

Area	Part used	Uses	References
Bagerhat district, Bangladesh	Leaf	Bone pain, body pain, fever, cough, mucus	Rahmatullah *et al.* (2010)
Jhang district, Pakistan	Seeds	Worm infestation	Badar *et al.* (2017)
Western Morang, Nepal	Leaf (decoction)	Joint swelling	Raut and Shrestha (2012)
Greater Cholistan desert (Pakistan)	Seed (infusion)	Arthritis and rheumatism	Khan (2009)
Greater Cholistan desert (Pakistan)	Leaf (dried)	Worm infestation	Khan (2009)
Hangu district, Pakistan	Seed, leaf	Rheumatism,	Tariq *et al.* (2016)
Mansehra district, Pakistan	Leaf	Mange	Sindhu *et al.* (201)
Kohat, Pakistan	Stem	Mange, stomach problems, fever	Tariq *et al.* (2014)
Karak district, Pakistan	Whole plant	Flatulence	Khattak *et al.* (2015)

6. Conclusions

Ethnoveterinary plants all across the world have been used to treat several diseases or ailments of animals. This extensive literature survey has shown tremendous ethnoveterinary applications of various parts such as leaf, stem, bark, flower and seed of *V. negundo*. It is found that *V. negundo* is used for treating several veterinary ailments or conditions such as fever, bone fracture, mastitis, foot and mouth disease, diarrhea, dysentery, bloating, dermatitis, worm infestation, snake bite, arthritis and joint swelling. The vast ethnoveterinary uses of *V. negundo* mentioned in this study may be fruitful for carrying out research on the plant that may come out with development of novel drugs that can be used against animal ailments.

7. References

1) Adhikary SP. Indigenous knowledge on animal health care practices in Surada block of Ganjam district, Odisha. European Journal of Environmental Ecology 2014; 1(1): 1-6.

2) Ahuja SC, Ahuja S, Ahuja A. Nirgundi (*Vitex negundo*) – Nature's gift to mankind. Asian Agri-History 2015; 19(1): 5-32.

3) Alagesaboopathi C. Medicinal plants used in the treatment of livestock diseases in Salem district, Tamilnadu, India. World Journal of Pharmaceutical Research 2015; 4(4): 829-836.

4) Badar N, Iqbal Z, Sajid MS, Rizwan HM, Jabbar A, Badar W, Khan MN, Ahmed A. Documentation of ethnoveterinary practices in district Jhang, Pakistan. The Journal of Animal & Plant Sciences 2017; 27(2): 398-406.

5) Baidya S, Thakur B, Devi A. Ethnomedicinal plants of the sacred groves and their uses by Karbi tribe in Karbi Anglong district of Assam, Northeast India. Indian Journal of Traditional Knowledge 2020; 19(2): 277-287.

6) Bandyopadhyay S, Mukherjee SK. Ethnoveterinary medicine from Koch Bihar district, West Bengal. Indian Journal of Traditional Knowledge 2005; 4(4): 456-461.

7) Bhatt A, Singh P Kumar V, Baunthiyal M. Documentation of Ethno - Veterinary Practices used for Treatments of Different Ailments in Garhwal Himalayan Region. Journal of Environmental Nanotechnology 2013; 2: 22-29.

8) Bhatt PR, Pandya KB, Patel UD, Patel HB, Modi CM. Survey on ethnoveterinary practices around Junagadh, Gujarat, India. Indian Journal of Pharmaceutical Sciences 2019; 81(1): 161-167.

9) Bhuvaneswari R, Ramanathan R, Mathumathi TK, Madheswaran A, Dhandapani R. Survey of ethno-veterinary medicinal plants in Namakkal district, Tamil Nadu, India. Journal of Medicinal Plants Studies 2015; 3(6): 33-45.

10) Deshmukh OS, Pochhi VU. Plants used in ethno-veterinary medicines by tribal peoples in Betul district, Madhya Pradesh, India. International Journal of Applied Research 2017; 3(3S): 34-39.

11) Devendrakumar D, Anbazhagan M. Ethnoveterinary medicinal plants used in Perambalur district, Tamil Nadu. Research in Plant Biology 2012; 2(3): 24-30.

12) Dhanam S, Elayaraj B. Ethnoveterinary practices in Villupuram district, Tamil Nadu, India. International Letters of Natural Sciences 2014; 19: 1-7.

13) Dhananjaya B, Vinod, Navinkumar, Shashidhara KK. Plant based ethno-veterinary medicine used by farmers in Udupi District of Karnataka. International Journal of Chemical Studies 2018; 6(2): 958-961.

14) Dharmasiri MG, Jayakody JR, Galhena G, Liyanage SS, Ratnasooriya WD. Anti-inflammatory and analgesic activities of mature fresh leaves of *Vitex negundo*. Journal of Ethnopharmacology 2003; 87(2-3): 199-206.

15) Dhore RK, Undal VS. Medico-botanical studies in relation to veterinary medicinal plant from Akola district, of Maharashtra. International Journal of Current Research 2017; 9(11): 61725-61731.

16) Ekka A. Plants used in ethno-veterinary medicine by Oraon tribals of north - east Chhattisgarh, India. World Journal of Pharmaceutical Research 2015; 4(9): 1038-1044.

17) Emmi SN. Herbal medicines for livestock health management used by Jende Kuruba community in Athani taluka of Belgaum district. International Journal of Science and Research 2015; 4(12): 2216-2217.

18) Gadpayale JV, Khobragade DP, Chaturvedi AA. Traditional ethno-veterinary practices in Bhandara district (M.S.) India. International Journal of Sciences and Applied Research 2014; 1(2): 91-99.

19) Galav P, Jain A, Katewa SS. Ethnoveterinary medicines used by tribals of Tadgarh-Raoli wildlife sanctuary, Rajasthan, India. Indian Journal of Traditional Knowledge 2013; 12(1): 56-61.

20) Ganesan S, Chandhirasekaran M, Selvaraj A. Ethnoveterinary healthcare practices in southern districts of Tamil Nadu. Indian Journal of Traditional Knowledge 2008; 7(2): 347-354.

21) Ganesan S, Pandi RN, Banumathy N. Ethnomedicinal survey of Alagarkoil hills (reserved forest), Tamil Nadu, India. eJournal of Indian Medicine 2007–2008; 1: 1-18.

22) Gayakvad P, Jadeja DB, Thakre B, Bhalawe S, Nayak D. Ethno-veterinary medicinal plants of mahal village of dang district, Gujarat, India. Research in Environment and Life Sciences 2014; 7(2): 99-100.

23) Guruprasad NM, Prasad DAG. Ethno veterinary medicinal plants and practices in Honnavar Taluk, North Kanara district of Karnataka. Journal of Drug Delivery and Therapeutics 2019; 9(3):117-120.

24) Harsha VH, Shripathi V, Hegde GR. Ethnoveterinary practices in Uttara Kannada district of Karnataka. Indian Journal of Traditional Knowledge 2005; 4(3): 253-258.

25) Holennavar PS, Kulkarni LC. Biodiversity and Strategies for Conservation of Ethnoveterinary Medicinal plants in Khanapur Taluka Gandigwad of

Belgaum District, Karnataka, India. International Journal for Innovative Research in Science & Technology 2015; 1(12): 225-231.

26) Jagadeeswary V, Reddy SM, Satyanarayan K. Ethno-veterinary practices used by tribals of Chittoor district, Andhra Pradesh, India. Indian Journal of Animal Research 2014; 48(3): 251-257.

27) Jambu S, Wath M. Survey and documentation of ethnoveterinary healthcare practices used by rural people of Akola district of Maharashtra. International Journal of Research – Granthaalayah 2018; 6(1): 306-318.

28) Jamwal JS, Kant S. Ethno-veterinary herbal practice in Kalakote range, Rajouri (J&K), India. Nature Environment and Pollution Technology 2008; 7(3): 571-572.

29) Jatav R, Krishna VK, Mehta R. Ethnoveterinary use of some medicinal plants of Shivpuri district (M.P.) India. Golden Research Thoughts 2014; 4(6): 1-5.

30) Jayakumar S, Baskaran N, Arumugam R, Sathiskumar S, Pugazhenthi M. Herbal medicine as a live practice for treating livestock ailments by indigenous people: A case study from the Konar community of Tamil Nadu. South African Journal of Botany 2018; 118: 23-32.

31) Kamruzzaman M, Bari SM, Faruque SM. *In vitro* and *in vivo* bactericidal activity of *Vitex negundo* leaf extract against diverse multidrug resistant enteric bacterial pathogens. Asian Pacific Journal of Tropical Medicine 2013; 6(5): 352-359.

32) Kannan M, Kumar ST, Rao MV. Ethnobotanical note on the veterinary health-care management by Malayali tribes of Kalrayan hills. Asian Journal of Pharmaceutical and Clinical Research 2016; 9(S1): 66-82.

33) Khan FM. Ethno-veterinary medicinal usage of flora of greater Cholistan desert (Pakistan). Pakistan Veterinary Journal 2009, 29(2): 75-80.

34) Khattak NS, Nouroz F, Ur Rahman I, Noreen S. Ethno veterinary uses of medicinal plants of district Karak, Pakistan. Journal of Ethnopharmacology 2015; 171: 273-279.

35) Kiruba S, Jeeva S, Dhas SSM. Enumeration of ethnoveterinary plants of Cape Comorin, Tamil Nadu. Indian Journal of Traditional Knowledge 2006; 5(4): 576-578.

36) Lenka KC, Pradhan N, Padhan B. Ethnoveterinary medicines: A Potential alternative to animal health care for the tribal communities of Koraput, Odisha. International Journal of Pharmacology, Phytochemistry and Ethnomedicine 2018; 11: 26-38.

37) Mairh AK, Mishra PK. Ethno-veterinary wisdom of Birhore tribes of Jharkhand. International Journal of Bioassays 2015; 4(2): 3686-3687.

38) Mallik BK, Panda T, Padhy RN. Ethnoveterinary practices of aborigine tribes in Odisha, India. Asian Pacific Journal of Tropical Biomedicine 2012; S1520-S1525.

39) Meen ML, Dudi A, Singh D. Ethnoveterinary study of medicinal plants in a tribal society of Marwar region of Rajasthan, India. Journal of Pharmacognosy and Phytochemistry 2020; 9(4): 549-554.

40) Meena DC, Garai S, Maiti S, Bhatt N, Meena BS. Ethno-veterinary practices followed by Raika pastoralists of Rajasthan: A descriptive study. Journal of Pharmacognosy and Phytochemistry 2020; 9(2): 63-66.

41) Meena KL. Some traditional ethno-veterinary plants of district Pratapgarh, Rajasthan, India. American Journal of Ethnomedicine 2014; 1(6): .393-401.

42) Mishra DP, Sahu RK, Mishra N, Behera AK. Herbal treatment for common diseases in ruminants: an overview. Journal of Livestock Science 2015; 6: 36-43.

43) Naik RM, Venugopalan V, Kumaravelayutham P, Krishnamurthy YL. Ethnoveterinary uses of medicinal plants among the Lambani community in Chitradurga district, Karnataka, India. Asian Pacific Journal of Tropical Biomedicine 2012; S470-S476.

44) Narayana LV, Narasimharao GM. Plants used in ethnoveterinary medicine by tribals of Visakhapatnam and Vizianagarm districts, Andhra Pradesh, India. International Journal of Pure and Applied Bioscience 2015; 3(2): 432-439.

45) Nimbalkar SD, Patil DS, Deo AD. Ethnoveterinary practices (EVP) for control of ectoparasite in livestock. Indian Journal of Traditional Knowledge 2020; 19(2): 401-405.

46) Panda T, Mishra N. Indigenous knowledge on animal health care practices in Kendrapara district of Odisha, India. International Letters of Natural Sciences 2016; 53: 10-27.

47) Parthiban R, Vijayakumar S, Prabhu S, Yabesh JGEM. Quantitative traditional knowledge of medicinal plants used to treat livestock diseases from Kudavasal taluk of Thiruvarur district, Tamil Nadu, India. Brazilian Journal of Pharmacognosy 2016; 26: 109-121.

48) Poornima G, Manasa M, Rudrappa D, Kekuda PTR. Medicinal plants used by herbal healers in Narasipura and Manchale villages of Sagara Taluk, Karnataka, India. Science, Technology and Arts Research Journal 2012; 1(2): 12-17.

49) Prakasha HM, Krishnappa M. People's knowledge on medicinal plants in Sringeri taluk, Karnataka. Indian Journal of Traditional Knowledge 2006; 5(3): 353-357.

50) Pranjale A, Dube KG. Ethno-veterinary traditional knowledge of some plants used in Wardha district (Maharashtra). International Journal of Science and Research 2016; 5(5): 1279-1283.

51) Preeti P, Solanki CM. Ethnoveterinary plants used against mastitis disease by different tribes of Nimar region Madhya Pradesh. International Journal of Botany Studies 2016; 1(6): 30-32.

52) Preeti P. Ethnoveterinary studies of plants used in retention of placenta of cattle in Nimar Region (M.P.). International Journal of Scientific Research in Science and Technology 2018; 4(1): 226-230.

53) Pushpangadan P, Ijinu TP, Bincy AJ, Anzar S, Aswany T, Chitra MA, Harsha K, Sreedevi P, George V. Traditional medicine in livestock management. Journal of Traditional and Folk Practices 2016; 2-4(1): 43-49.

54) Radha, Puri S, Janjua S, Srivastava S, Neg V. Some commonly used wild ethnoveterinary medicinal plants by migratory shepherds in churdhar wildlife sanctuary of district Sirmaur in Himachalpradesh, India. Plant Archives 2020; 20(Special Issue AIAAS-2020): 136-138.

55) Rahaman CH, Ghosh A, Mandal S. Studies on the Ethno-veterinary medicinal plants used by the tribals of Birbhum district, West Bengal. In: Singh V (Editor), Ethnobotany and Medicinal Plants of India and Nepal (Vol. 3), Scientific Publisher (India), Jodhpur, 2009, Pp 333-338.

56) Rahmatullah M, Mollik MAH, Alam MJ, Ahmmed B, Jahan FI, Sintaha M, Khaleque HN, Chowdhury MH, Noor FA, Rahman S, Jahan R, Seraj S. An ethnoveterinary survey of medicinal plants used by folk medicinal practitioners to treat cattle diseases in randomly selected areas of Bagerhat district, Bangladesh. American-Eurasian Journal of Sustainable Agriculture 2010; 4(3): 386-396.

57) Rajkumari R, Nirmala RK, Singh PK, Das AK, Dutta BK, Pinokiyo A. Ethnoveterinary plants used by the Chiru tribes of Manipur, Northeast India. Indian Journal of Traditional Knowledge 2014; 13(2): 368-376.

58) Ramana VM. Ethnomedicinal and ethnoveterinary plants from Boath, Adilabad district, Andhra Pradesh, India. Ethnobotanical Leaflets 2008; 12: 391-400.

59) Ranganathan V. Ethno veterinary practices for combating antimicrobial resistance. International Journal of Science, Environment and Technology 2017; 6(1): 840-844.

60) Raut B, Shrestha AP. Ethnoveterinary practices in western Morang, Nepal. International Journal of Pharmaceutical Sciences and Research 2012; 3(1): 182-188

61) Sadangi N, Sahu RK. Traditional veterinary herbal practice of Kalahandi district, Orissa, India. Journal of Natural Remedies 2004; 4(2): 131-136.

62) Saha MR, De Sarker D, Sen A. Ethnoveterinary practices among the tribal community of Malda district of West Bengal, India. Indian Journal of Traditional Knowledge 2014; 13(2): 359-367.

63) Saini JS, Sood SK. Plants Used for Ethnoveterinary Care by Gujjars in and around Colonel Sher Jung National Park Simbalbara, Sirmour, Himachal Pradesh, India. International Journal of Research 2018; 7(8): 560-569.

64) Sasikala V, Tiwari R, Saravanan M. Ethno-veterinary practices for disease conditions of goat in Bareilly district (Uttar Pradesh). International Journal of Science, Environment and Technology 2018; 7(3): 973-977.

65) Satapathy KB. Ethnoveterinary practices in Jajpur district of Orissa. Indian Journal of Traditional Knowledge 2010; 9(2): 338-343.

66) Selvi SS, Kumar JS, Balasubramaniam V. Studies on the ethnoveterinary medicinal plants among the farmers of Dharapuram taluk, Tirupur district, Tamil Nadu. Konganadu Research Journal 2015; 2(2): 155-159.

67) Seyoum Y, Teketay D, Shumi G, Wodafirash M. Edible wild fruit trees and shrubs and their socioeconomic significance in Central Ethiopia. Ethnobotany Research and Applications 2015; 14: 183-197.

68) Sharma R, Manhas RK, Magotra R. Ethnoveterinary remedies of diseases among milk yielding animals in Kathua, Jammu and Kashmir, India. Journal of Ethnopharmacology 2012; 141: 265-272.

69) Sikarwar RLS, Kumar V. Ethnoveterinary knowledge and practices prevalent among the tribals of central India. Journal of Natural Remedies 2005; 5(2): 147-152.

70) Sikarwar RLS, Tiwari AP. A review of plants used in ethnoveterinary medicine in Central India. Indian Journal of Traditional Knowledge 2020; 19(3): 617-634.

71) Sindhu ZUD, Iqbal Z, Khan MN, Jonsson NN, Siddique M. Documentation of ethnoveterinary practices used for treatment of different ailments in a selected hilly area of Pakistan. International Journal of Agriculture and Biology 2010; 12(3): 353-358.

72) Singh B, Singh B, Kishor A, Singh S, Bhat MN, Surmal O, Musarella CM. Exploring plant-based ethnomedicine and quantitative ethnopharmacology: Medicinal plants utilized by the population of Jasrota hill in Western Himalaya. Sustainability 2020; 12: 7526.

73) Siva V, Ramesh V, Mhalingam P. Ethno-veterinary survey of medicinal plants in Kovilpatti taluk, Tuticorin district, Tamil Nadu, India. International Journal of Current Science Research 2016; 2(9): 901-915.

74) Sreenivasa and Kumar. Educational training on ethno veterinary: uses and application of medicinal plants of traditional livestock healers. Global Journal of Bio-Science and Biotechnology 2017; 6(4): 582-587.

75) Sumeet D, Abhishek D, Paras G. Role of plants as veterinary medicine from Madhya Pradesh, India: A status survey. Journal of Pharmacy Research 2009; 2(4): 688-690.

76) Tariq A, Adnan M, Mussarat S. Use of ethnoveterinary medicines by the people living near Pak-Afghan border region. Slovenian Veterinary Research 2016; 53 (3): 119-130.

77) Tariq A, Mussarat S, Adnan M, AbdElsalam NM, Ullah R, Khan AL. Ethnoveterinary study of medicinal plants in a tribal society of Sulaiman range. Scientific World Journal 2014; 2014: 127526.

78) Tendon VR. Medicinal uses and biological activities of *Vitex negundo*. Natural Product Radiance 2005; 5(3): 162-165.

79) Upadhyay B, Singh KP, Kumar A. Ethno-veterinary uses and informants consensus factor of medicinal plants of Sariska region, Rajasthan, India. Journal of Ethnopharmacology 2011; 133: 14-25.

80) Verma RK. An ethnobotanical study of plants used for the treatment of livestock diseases in Tikamgarh district of Bundelkhand, Central India. Asian Pacific Journal of Tropical Biomedicine 2014; 4(Suppl 1): S460-S467.

81) Vinothraj S, Alagesan P, Siva M. Ethno-veterinary practices adaptation for management of poultry diseases in Erode district. International Journal of Current Microbiology and Applied Sciences 2019; 8(4): 2758-2761.

82) Zheng CJ, Li HQ, Ren SC, Xu CL, Rahman K, Qin LP, Sun YH. Phytochemical and pharmacological profile of *Vitex negundo*. Phytotherapy Research 2015; 29(5): 633-647.

Cite this chapter as:

Kekuda PTR, Mahalakshmi SN. Ethnoveterinary potential of *Vitex negundo* L. (Lamiaceae) – A review. In: Kekuda PTR, Vinayaka KS, Raghavendra HL (Editors), Nature and Medicine: Traditional uses, chemistry and bioprospecting of natural products. JPS Scientific Publications, Tamil Nadu, India, 2020, Pp 88 - 100.

Nature and Medicine: Traditional Uses, Chemistry and Bioprocessing of Natural Products
ISBN: 978-81-947154-3-6
First Edition; 2020
Chapter – 10, Page: 101 - 111

10

ANTIOXIDANT ACTIVITY OF
Mimusops elengi L.
(Sapotaceae) FRUIT

Ramyashree K. R[1,2], Achala H. G[1,3], Pramod G[1], Prashith Kekuda T. R[1*]

[1]Department of Microbiology, S.R.N.M.N College of Applied Sciences, NES Campus, Balraj Urs road,
Shivamogga – 577 201, Karnataka, India
[2]Division of Biochemistry, J.S.S.A.H.E.R, Banni Mantap, Mysuru-570015, Karnataka, India
[3]P.G. Department of Studies and Research in Biochemistry, Jnana Sahyadri, Kuvempu University,
Shankaraghatta – 577 451, Karnataka, India

*Corresponding author: p.kekuda@gmail.com

Abstract

In this study, the methanolic extract of *Mimusops elengi* L. (Sapotaceae) fruit was screened for *in vitro* antifungal activity by DPPH, ABTS and ferric reducing assays. The fruit extract scavenged DPPH and ABTS radicals dose dependently with an IC_{50} value of 21.15 µg/ml and 34.43 µg/ml, respectively. An increase in the absorbance on increasing the concentration of extract indicated reducing potential of fruit extract. In conclusion, consumption of the fruits of *M. elengi* can be helpful to manage oxidative damage induced by free radicals.

Key words: *Mimusops elengi*, DPPH, ABTS and Ferric reducing.

1. Introduction

Oxygen is crucial for life, however reactive oxygen species such as superoxide radical, hydroxyl radical, singlet oxygen and hydrogen peroxide that are formed during metabolism pose threat to health under certain conditions. The ROS are known to adversely affect biomolecules such as proteins, lipids and nucleic acids

leading to oxidative damage. Several diseases/disorders such as ageing, cancer, cardiovascular diseases and neurodegenerative diseases are associated with oxidative stress. Antioxidant enzymes such as catalase and superoxide dismutase and non-enzymatic antioxidants such as vitamin C, vitamin E and glutathione helps to overcome toxic effects of ROS. However, there is an extra need for antioxidants (from exogenous source) under certain conditions. Higher plants are shown to be one of the best resources of dietary antioxidants. Polyphenolic compounds from plants appears to be promising antioxidant agents (Aiyegoro and Okoh, 2010; Ebrahimzadeh *et al.*, 2010; Shahwar and Raza, 2012; Kekuda *et al.*, 2013; Youn *et al.*, 2019).

Mimusops elengi L. (Sapotaceae) is a medium sized evergreen tree and one the important medicinal plants used traditionally for various purposes in several countries. The plant is commonly known as Indian Medlar or bullet wood in English and Bakula in Sanskrit. *M. elengi* is used in indigenous systems of medicine such as Ayurveda and Unani. The fruits of *M. elengi* are edible and the timber is valuable. Flowers are used to make garland. The plant is used traditionally as dye and for treating teeth problems, urinary problems, fever, diarrhea, dysentery, pyorrhea, dizziness, sexually transmitted diseases, diabetes, skin disorders and headache (Mitra, 1981; Sadangi and Sahu, 2004; Alagesaboopathi, 2009; Sahu *et al.*, 2011; Gami *et al.*, 2012; Das and Teron, 2014; Rout and Panda, 2010; Ayyanar and Ignacimuthu, 2011; Chakraborty and Paul, 2014; Maneenoon *et al.*, 2015; Sekar *et al.*, 2016; Shiva *et al.*, 2017; Rani and Rahman, 2017; Chetia and Das, 2018; Hemila and Krishnaveni, 2019; Sahnmugam *et al.*, 2020; Atre and Khedkar, 2020; Kyaw *et al.*, 2021). *M. elengi* is shown to exhibit bioactivities such as antibacterial (Sircar and Mandal, 2016), antifungal (Satish *et al.*, 2008), antioxidant (Vinay *et al.*, 2016), cytotoxic (Natungnuy and Poeaim, 2018), analgesic (Karmakar *et al.*, 2011), antiurolithiatic (Ashok *et al.*, 2010), antihyperglycemic (Ganu *et al.*, 2010), wound healing (Gupta and Jain, 2011), molluscicidal (Singh *et al.*, 2012), anti-inflammatory (Purnima *et al.*, 2010), antipyretic (Purnima *et al.*, 2010), antiulcer (Shah *et al.*, 2003) and anti-anxiety activity (Ganu *et al.*, 2011). In this study, we investigated antiradical and reducing properties of methanolic extract of *M. elengi* fruit.

2. Materials and Methods

2.1. Collection and extraction

The fruits of *M. elengi* (Figure - 1) were collected at Hosagunda, Shivamogga district, Karnataka during December 2018 and identified by Dr. Vinayaka K.S., Assistant Professor, Department of Botany, S.V.S College, Bantwal, Dakshina Kannada, Karnataka.The fruits were washed, dried under shade, powdered and

extracted by maceration process using methanol as menstruum (Dhanya Shree *et al.*, 2018). The crude fruit extract was tested for detection of phytochemical groups by standard procedures (Tiwari *et al.*, 2011; Jamil *et al.*, 2012).

Figure - 1: Fruits of *M. elengi* (Photograph by Vinayaka K.S)

2.2. Preparation of fruit extract for Antioxidant activity

The fruit extract was diluted in methanol to obtain different concentrations ranging from 3.12 to 50 μg extract/ml of methanol. The ascorbic acid (reference standard) was also prepared in the same manner.

2.3. Antioxidant activity of fruit extract

2.3.1. DPPH free radical scavenging of fruit extract

One ml of each concentration of extract/ascorbic acid was added to 3 ml of DPPH radical solution (0.004 %), incubated in dark for 20 minutes followed by measuring the absorbance at 520 nm. The extent of scavenging of DPPH radicals (%) and IC_{50} values were calculated (Kekuda *et al.*, 2013).

2.3.2. ABTS radical scavenging of fruit extract

One ml of each concentration of extract/ascorbic acid was added to 3 ml of ABTS radical solution, incubated in dark for about 20 minutes followed by measuring the absorbance at 734nm. The extent of scavenging of ABTS radicals (%) and the IC_{50} values were calculated (Kekuda *et al.*, 2013).

2.3.3. Ferric reducing activity of fruit extract

The reaction mixtures consisting of 1ml of various concentrations of fruit extract/ascorbic acid, 2.5 ml phosphate buffer (pH 6.6) and 2.5 ml of Potassium ferricyanide (1 %) were incubated at 50 °C in a water bath for 20 minutes followed by cooling. A volume of 2.5 ml of trichloroacetic acid (10 %) was added followed by 0.5ml of ferric chloride (0.1 %). Absorbance of reaction mixtures was measured at 700 nm after an incubation of 10 minutes at room temperature (Kekuda *et al.*, 2013).

3. Results and Discussion

3.1. Phytochemicals detected in the fruit extract

Maceration is one of the simple extraction procedures used for getting plant extracts using appropriate solvents. Methanol is one of the polar solvents extensively used for extraction as methanol is shown to extract more number of phytochemicals (Tiwari *et al.*, 2011; Chigayo *et al.*, 2016; Dhawan and Gupta, 2017). Phytochemical analysis of the fruit extract identified tannins, saponins, flavonoids, glycosides and triterpenes.

3.2. DPPH radical scavenging activity of fruit extract

DPPH is a stable, purple colored, organic free radical which on accepting a proton from an antioxidant becomes DPPHH (diphenylpicryl hydrazyl) which is yellow in color. The assay that involves scavenging of stable DPPH radicals has been employed to determine antiradical potential of various botanical extracts (Wangcharoen and Morasuk, 2007; Aiyegoro and Okoh, 2010; Ebrahimzadeh *et al.*, 2010; Kekuda *et al.*, 2013; Felhi *et al.*, 2017; Dhanya Shree *et al.*, 2018). The extract was effective in displaying concentration dependent scavenging of DPPH radicals with an IC_{50} value of 21.15 µg/ml. The fruit extract scavenged radicals to 50 % and higher at concentration 25 µg/ml and higher (Figure - 2). Ascorbic acid was more effective in scavenging DPPH radicals (IC_{50} value of 7.19 µg/ml). Valve *et al.* (2011) revealed DPPH radical scavenging potential of various solvent extracts of *M. elengi* fruits with marked activity being displayed by acetone extract. The study of Boonyuen *et al.* (2009) revealed scavenging of DPPH radicals by crude extract from ripe fruits of *M. elengi* was lower when compared to immature and mature extracts. DPPH scavenging potential of crude extract of leaves (Saha *et al.*, 2008; Karmakar *et al.*, 2011) and stem bark (Rao *et al.*, 2011; Shahwar and Raza, 2012) of *M. elengi* was reported. A polyherbal formulation containing *M. elengi* scavenged DPPH radicals with an IC_{50} value of 45.16µg/ml (Poongodi and Nazeema, 2019).

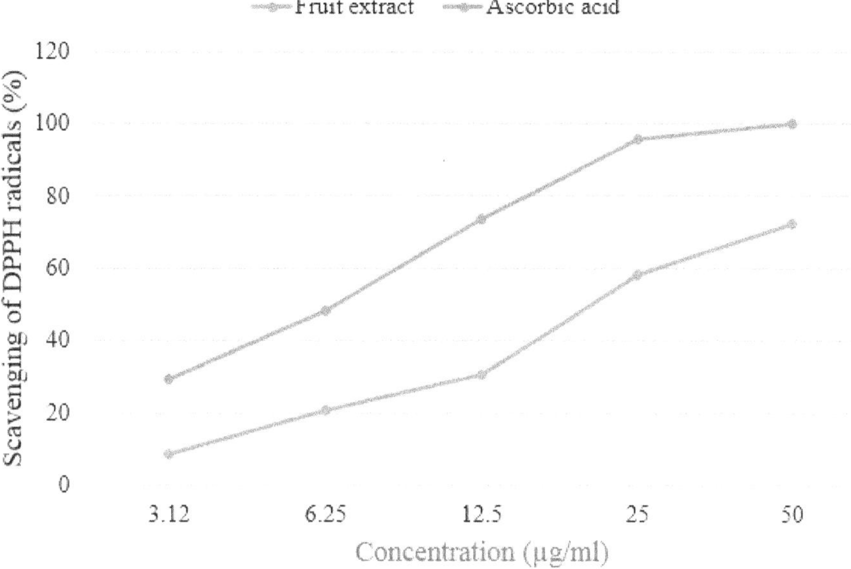

Figure - 2: scavenging of DPPH radicals by fruit extracts

3.3. ABTS radical scavenging activity of fruit extract

The scavenging of the ABTS radicals by compounds having hydrogen-donating potential (antioxidants) is measured by the decrease of its characteristic long wave absorption spectrum which is measured at 734nm. ABTS scavenging activity has been routinely used to evaluate antiradical potential of chain breaking antioxidants including botanicals (Wangcharoen and Morasuk, 2007; Teow *et al.*, 2007; Camacho-Luis *et al.*, 2008; Aiyegoro and Okoh, 2010; Kekuda *et al.*, 2013; Felhi *et al.*, 2017; Gulcin, 2020). The fruit extract of *M. elengi* displayed dose dependent scavenging of ABTS radicals with scavenging activity of 50 % and higher shown at extract concentration of 50 µg (Figure - 3). Ascorbic acid scavenged radicals with an IC_{50} value of 6.08 µg/ml which was found to be lesser than that of fruit extract (IC_{50} value of 34.43 µg/ml). In an earlier study, Boonyuen *et al.* (2009) revealed scavenging of ABTS radicals by crude extract from ripe fruits of *M. elengi* was lower when compared to immature and mature extracts. The study carried out by Natungnuy and Poeaim (2018) showed DPPH radical scavenging potential of methanolic extract of flowers of *M. elengi* with an IC_{50} value of 98.20 µg/ml. The study of Rao *et al.* (2011) revealed dose dependent scavenging of ABTS radicals by chloroform extract of bark of *M. elengi*. A polyherbal formulation containing *M. elengi* was effective in displaying dose dependent scavenging of ABTS radicals (Poongodi and Nazeema, 2019).

Chapter - 10

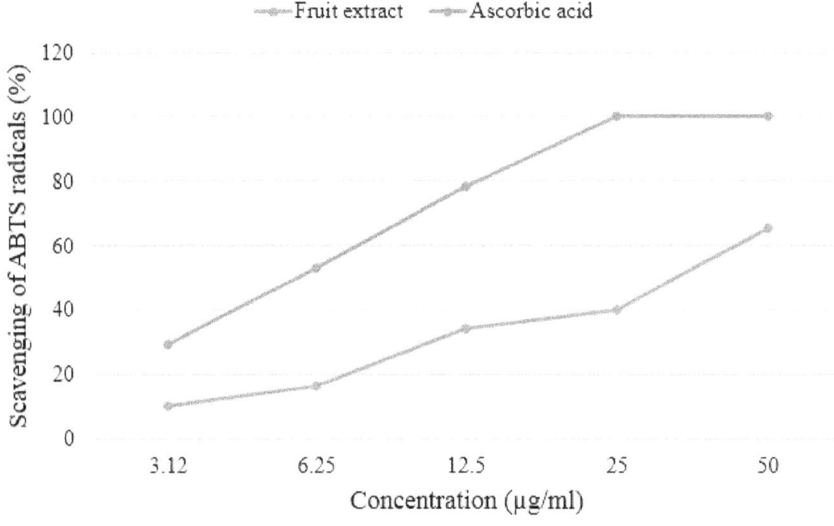

Figure - 3: ABTS free radical scavenging of fruit extract

3.4. Ferric reducing activity of fruit extract

The reducing capacity is a significant indicator of antioxidant activity of a substance and is related to the presence of reductones. The assay that involves reduction of Fe^{3+} to Fe^{2+} is routinely employed evaluate antioxidant potential of botanicals (Ebrahimzadeh *et al.*, 2010; Kekuda *et al.*, 2013; Dhanya Shree *et al.*, 2018). In this study, the fruit extract displayed reducing property as indicated by an increase in absorbance with increase in the concentration of extract (Figure 4). In the earlier studies, Saha *et al.* (2008), Uddin *et al.* (2018) showed reducing potential of leaf extract of *M. elengi*.

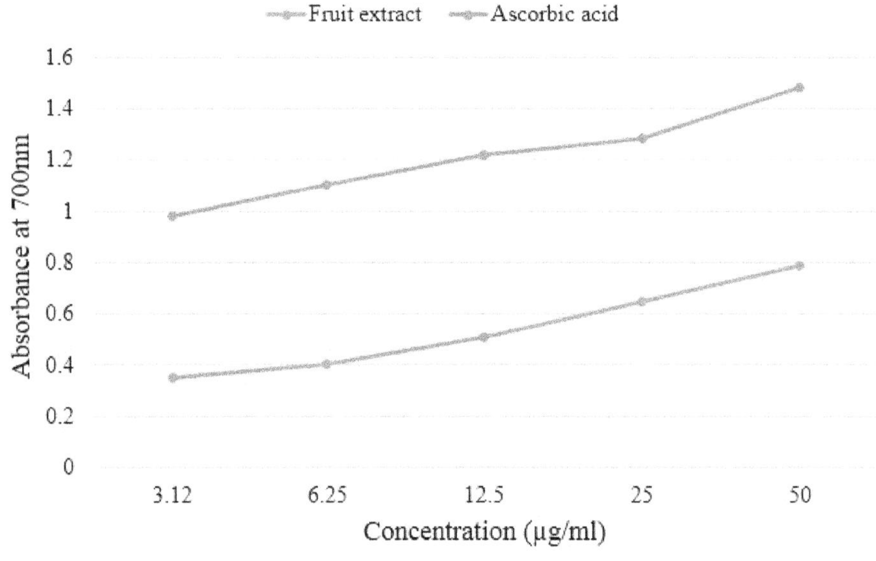

Figure - 4: ferric reducing efficacy of fruit extracts

4. Conclusions

The present study highlighted antioxidant potential of fruit extract of *M. elengi* which can be related to flavonoids and phenolic compounds. Hence, consuming fruits of *M. elengi* appears to be beneficial with respect to combating the deleterious effects of free radicals in addition to nutritive benefits.

Acknowledgements

Authors would like to thank Head, Dept. of Microbiology and Principal, S.R.N.M.N College of Applied Sciences and N.E.S, Shivamogga for providing facilities and moral support to conduct the work. Authors thank Dr. Vinayaka K.S for assisting in collection and identification of fruit.

5. References

1) Aiyegoro OA, Okoh AI. Preliminary phytochemical screening and *In vitro* antioxidant activities of the aqueous extract of *Helichrysum longifolium* DC BMC Complementary and Alternative Medicine 2010; 10: 21.

2) Alagesaboopathi C. Ethnomedicinal plants and their utilization by villagers in Kumaragiri Hills of Salem district of Tamilnadu, India. African Journal of Traditional, Complementary and Alternative Medicine 2009; 6(3): 222-227.

3) Ashok P, Koti BC, Vishwanathswamy AH. Antiurolithiatic and antioxidant activity of *Mimusops elengi* on ethylene glycol-induced urolithiasis in rats. Indian Journal of Pharmacology 2010; 42(6): 380-383.

4) Atre NM, Khedkar DD. A review on herbal remedies for sexually transmitted infections (STIs) from Melghat region of Maharashtra State, India. European Journal of Medicinal Plants 2020; 31(14): 1-17.

5) Ayyanar M, Ignacimuthu S. Ethnobotanical survey of medicinal plants commonly used by Kani tribals in Tirunelveli hills of Western Ghats, India. Journal of Ethnopharmacology 2011; 134: 851-864.

6) Boonyuen C, Wangkarn S, Suntornwat O, Chaisuksant R. Antioxidant capacity and phenolic content of *Mimusops elengi* fruit extract. Kasetsart Journal (Natural Science) 2009; 43: 21-27.

7) Camacho-Luis A, Gayosso-De-Lucio JA, Torres-Valencia JM, Munoz-Sanchez JL, Alarcon-Hernandez E, Lopez R, Barron BL. Antioxidant constituents of *Geranium bellum* Rose. Journal of the Mexican Chemical Society 2008; 52(2): 103-107.

8) Chakraborty NR, Paul A. Traditional knowledge on medicinal plants used by the tribal people of Birbhum district of West Bengal in India. International Journal of Agriculture, Environment and Biotechnology 2014; 7(3): 547-554.

9) Chetia DR, Das AK. Diversity of ethnomedicinal plants used by mising tribe of Dhemaji district, Assam. International Journal of Advanced Research 2018; 6(3): 815-825.

10) Chigayo K, Mojapelo PEL, Mnyakeni-Moleele S, Misihairabgwi JM. Phytochemical and antioxidant properties of different solvent extracts of *Kirkia wilmsii* tubers. Asian Pacific Journal of Tropical Biomedicine 2016; 6(12): 1037-1043.

11) Das C, Teron R. Ethnobotanical notes of the Rabha community in Mataikhar reserve forest of Kamrup district, Assam, India. Research Journal of Recent Science 2014; 3(6): 26-33.

12) Dhanya Shree VS, Ayesha A, Noorain SGK, Sahana BK, Kekuda PTR. Preliminary phytochemical analysis, antimicrobial and antioxidant activity of *Smilax zeylanica* L. (Smilacaceae). Journal of Drug Delivery Therapeutics 2018; 8(4):237-243.

13) Dhawan D, Gupta J. Comparison of different solvents for phytochemical extraction potential from *Datura metel* plant leaves. International Journal of Biological Chemistry 2017; 11: 17-22.

14) Ebrahimzadeh MA, Nabavi SM, Nabavi SF, Eslami B. Antioxidant activity of the bulb and aerial parts of *Ornithogalum sintenisii* L (Liliaceae) at flowering stage. Tropical Journal of Pharmaceutical Research 2010; 9(2): 141-148.

15) Felhi S, Daoud A, Hajlaoui H, Mnafgui K, Gharsallah N, Kadri A. Solvent extraction effects on phytochemical constituents profiles, antioxidant and antimicrobial activities and functional group analysis of *Ecballium elaterium* seeds and peels fruits. Food Science and Technology 2017; 37(3): 483-492.

16) Gami B, Pathak S, Parabia M. Ethnobotanical, phytochemical and pharmacological review of *Mimusops elengi* Linn. Asian Pacific Journal of Tropical Biomedicine 2012; 2(9): 743-748.

17) Ganu G, Garud A, Agarwal V, Suralkar U, Jadhav S, Kshirsagar A. Anti-anxiety activity of *Mimusops elengi* barks extract in experimental animals. Research Journal of Pharmaceutical, Biological and Chemical Sciences 2011; 2(3): 405-410.

18) Ganu GP, Jadhav SS, Deshpande AD. Antioxidant and antihyperglycemic potential of methanolic extract of bark of *Mimusops elengi* L. in mice. Research Journal of Pharmaceutical, Biological and Chemical Sciences 2010; 1(3): 67-77.

19) Gulcin İ. Antioxidants and antioxidant methods: an updated overview. Archives of Toxicology 2020; 94(3): 651-715.

20) Gupta N, Jain UK. Investigation of wound healing activity of methanolic extract of stem bark of *Mimusops elengi* Linn. African Journal of Traditional, Complementary and Alternative Medicine 2011; 8(2): 98-103.

21) Hemila P, Krishnaveni C. Survey of ethno medicinal plants, Nilgiri biosphere nature park at Thuvaipathy, Anaikatti, Coimbatore, Tamilnadu, India. Plant Archives 2019; 19(1): 441-448.

22) Jamil M, Mirza B, Yasmeen A, Khan MA. Pharmacological activities of selected plant species and their phytochemical analysis. Journal of Medicinal Plants Research 2012; 6(37): 5013-5022.

23) Karmakar UK, Sultana R, Biswas NN. Antioxidant, analgesic and cytotoxic activities of *Mimusops elengi* Linn. leaves. International Journal of Pharmaceutical Sciences and Research 2011; 2(11): 2791-2797.

24) Kekuda PTR, Manasa M, Poornima G, Abhipsa V, Rekha C, Upashe SP, Raghavendra HL. Antibacterial, cytotoxic and antioxidant potential of *Vitex negundo* var. *negundo* and *Vitex negundo* var. *purpurascens*- A comparative study. Science, Technology and Arts Research Journal 2013; 2(3): 59-68.

25) Kyaw YMM, Bi Y, Oo TN, Yang X. Traditional medicinal plants used by the Mon people in Myanmar. Journal of Ethnopharmacology 2021; 265: 113253.

26) Maneenoon K, Khuniad C, Teanuan Y, Saedan N, Prom-In S, Rukleng N, Kongpool W, Pinsook P, Wongwiwat W. Ethnomedicinal plants used by traditional healers in Phatthalung Province, Peninsular Thailand. Journal of Ethnobiology and Ethnomedicine 2015; 11: 43.

27) Mitra R. Bakula – A reputed drug of Ayurveda, its history, uses in Indian medicine. Indian Journal of History of Science 1981; 16(2): 169-180.

28) Natungnuy K, Poeaim S. Antioxidant and cytotoxic activities of methanolic extracts from *Mimusops elengi* flowers. International Journal of Agricultural Technology 2018; 14(5):731-740.

29) Poongodi T, Nazeema TH. Evaluation of free radical scavenging and reducing power of polyherbal formulation comprising of three selected plants. International Research Journal of Pharmacy 2019; 10(4): 143-149.

30) Purnima A, Koti BC, Thippeswamy AH, Jaji MS, Swamy AH, Kurhe YV, Sadiq AJ. Antiinflammatory, analgesic and antipyretic activities of *Mimusops elengi* Linn. Indian Journal of Pharmaceutical Sciences 2010; 72(4): 480-485.

31) Rani S, Rahman K. Molsari (*Mimusops elengi* Linn.): A boon drug of traditional medicine. International Journal of Pharmaceutical Sciences and Research 2017; 8(1): 17-28.

32) Rao KS, Manjuluri PR, Keshar NK. *In vitro* antioxidant activity and total phenolic content of *Mimusops elengi* bark. Indian Journal of Pharmaceutical Education and Research 2011; 45(4): 317-323.

33) Rout SD, Panda SK. Ethnomedicinal plant resources of Mayurbhanj district, Orissa. Indian Journal of Traditional Knowledge 2010; 9(1): 68-72.

34) Sadangi N, Sahu RK. Traditional veterinary herbal practice of Kalahandi district, Orissa, India. Journal of Natural Remedies 2004; 4: 131-136.

35) Saha MR, Hasan SMR, Akter R, Hossain MM, Alam MS, Alam MA, Mazumder MEH. *In vitro* free radical scavenging activity of methanol extract of the leaves of *Mimusops elengi* Linn. Bangladesh Journal of Veterinary Medicine 2008; 6(2): 197-202.

36) Sahu SC, Pattnaik SK, Sahoo SL, Lenka SS, Dhal NK. Ethnobotanical study of medicinal plants in the coastal districts of Odisha. Current Botany 2011; 2(7): 17-20.

37) Satish S, Raghavendra MP, Mohana DC, Raveesha KA. Antifungal activity of a known medicinal plant *Mimusops elengi* L. against grain moulds. Journal of Agricultural Technology 2008; 4(1): 151-165.

38) Sekar K, Murugan K, Pandikumar P, Al-Sohaibani S, Ignacimuthu S. Anticaries potential of ethnomedicinal plants used by Malayali tribals from Kolli hills, India. Indian Journal of Traditional Knowledge 2016; 15(1): 109-115.

39) Shah PJ, Gandhi MS, Shah MB, Goswami SS, Santani D. Study of *Mimusops elengi* bark in experimental gastric ulcers. Journal of Ethnopharmacology 2003; 89(2-3): 305-311.

40) Shahwar D, Raza MA. Antioxidant potential of phenolic extracts of *Mimusops elengi*. Asian Pacific Journal of Tropical Biomedicine 2012; 2(7): 547-550.

41) Shanmugam S, Jeyaprabakaran G, Rajendran K. Medicinal trees from home gardens of urban areas in Madurai District of Tamil Nadu, Southern India. Asian Journal of Ethnobiology 2020; 3(1): 10-15.

42) Shiva B, Bhargav V, Nimbolkar PK. Under-exploited and nutritionally rich wild fruits of Telangana, India. International Journal of Current Microbiology and Applied Sciences 2017; 6(6): 2682-2694.

43) Singh KL, Singh DK, Singh VK. Characterization of the molluscicidal activity of *Bauhinia variegata* and *Mimusops elengi* plant extracts against the fasciola vector *Lymnaea acuminata*. Journal of the Institute of Tropical Medicine of São Paulo 2012; 54(3): 135-140.

44) Sircar B, Mandal S. Antibacterial activity of *Mimusops elengi* leaf, seed and bark extracts alone and in combination with antibiotics against human pathogenic bacteria. Translational Medicine (Sunnyvale) 2016; 6: 187.

45) Teow CC, Truong V, McFeeters RF, Thompson RL, Pecota KV, Yencho CG. Antioxidant activities, phenolic and b-carotene contents of sweet potato genotypes with varying flesh colours. Food Chemistry 2007; 103: 829-838.

46) Tiwari P, Kumar B, Kaur M, Kaur G, Kaur H. Phytochemical screening and extraction: A review. Internationale Pharmaceutica Sciencia 2011; 1(1): 98-106.

47) Uddin MM, Mostari F, Yeasmin S, Jalil MA, Akter N, Amin R, Islam MB. Evaluation of *in vitro* free radical scavenging and antioxidant activities of *Mimusops elengi* (Bokul) leaf extract. International Journal of Innovative Pharmaceutical Sciences and Research 2018; 6(9): 19-29.

48) Valvi SR, Rathod VS, Yesane DP. Screening of three wild edible fruits for their antioxidant Potential. Current Botany 2011; 2(1): 48-52.

49) Vinay KN, Lakshmi VV, Satyanarayan ND, Anantacharya R. *In vitro* antioxidant activity of leaf solvent extracts *Mimusops elengi* Linn. Journal of Medicinal Plants Studies 2016; 4(2): 84-87.

50) Wangcharoen W, Morasuk W. Antioxidant capacity and phenolic content of some Thai culinary plants. Maejo International Journal of Science and Technology 2007; 1(2): 100-106.

51) Youn JS, Kim YJ, Na HJ, Jung HR, Song CK, Kang SY, Kim JY. Antioxidant activity and contents of leaf extracts obtained from *Dendropanax morbifera* LEV are dependent on the collecting season and extraction conditions. Food Science and Biotechnology 2019; 28(1): 201-207.

Cite this chapter as:

Ramyashree KR, Achala HG, Pramod G, Kekuda PTR. Antioxidant activity of *Mimusops elengi* L. (Sapotaceae) fruit. In: Kekuda PTR, Vinayaka KS, Raghavendra HL (Editors), Nature and Medicine: Traditional uses, chemistry and bioprospecting of natural products. JPS Scientific Publications, Tamil Nadu, India, 2020, Pp 101 - 111.

Chapter - 10

Nature and Medicine: Traditional Uses, Chemistry and Bioprocessing of Natural Products
ISBN: 978-81-947154-3-6
First Edition; 2020
Chapter – 11, Page: 112 - 119

11

In vitro ANTIBACTERIAL ACTIVITY OF FRUTICOSE MACROLICHENS OF KARNATAKA, INDIA

Vinayaka K. S[1] and Prashith Kekuda T. R[2*]

[1]Department of Botany, Sri Venkataramana Swamy College, Bantwal-574211, Dakshina Kannada, Karnataka, India

[2]Department of Microbiology, S.R.N.M.N College of Applied Sciences, NES Campus, Balraj Urs road, Shivamogga – 577 201, Karnataka, India

*Corresponding author: p.kekuda@gmail.com

Abstract

Lichens are one of the examples for symbiotic association between a photosynthetic partner and a fungal partner. In the present study, we screened antibacterial efficacy of four fruticose macrolichens viz. *Usnea aciculifera* Vain., *Ramalina conduplicans* Vain., *Ramalina nervulosa* (Müll. Arg.) Abbayes, and *Teloschistes flavicans* (Sw.) Norman. The methanolic extracts of selected lichens (obtained by maceration process) were tested for antibacterial activity by agar well diffusion method. Extract from all lichen species tested were effective in showing inhibitory activity against bacteria. Among lichens, marked antibacterial activity was shown by *R. conduplicans*. Among test bacteria, *Bacillus subtilis* and *Escherichia coli* were shown to be susceptible to higher extent in case of Gram positive and Gram negative bacteria, respectively. The lichens selected for this study can be utilized in suitable form to treat infectious diseases caused by bacteria.

Key words: Macrolichens, Fruticose, Maceration, Antibacterial and Agar well diffusion.

1. Introduction

The wellbeing of humans is challenged by a variety of pathogens such as viruses, bacteria, fungi and protozoa. Bacteria cause a number of diseases in humans resulting in considerable morbidity and mortality. Although, antibiotics have been considered as the treatment of choice, they fail in most instances because of the development of resistance in pathogenic bacteria in a short span of time. This results in difficulty in treating the infectious diseases. Pathogens such as *Mycobacterium tuberculosis*, *Staphylococcus aureus*, *Enterobacter aerogenes*, *Pseudomonas aeruginosa*, *Escherichia coli* and *Acinetobacter* species are few of the common resistant bacterial pathogens. These resistant strains are common in hospital and community settings (Manchanda *et al.*, 2010; Kumar *et al.*, 2013; Reygaert, 2018; Aslam *et al.*, 2018). An intensified research has been undertaken by researchers on development of novel antibacterial activity from natural resources. Plants, lichens and their metabolites offer a promising resources of bioactive agents having activity against pathogenic bacteria including antibiotic resistant bacteria (Basappa and Venu Gopal, 2013; Kambar *et al.*, 2014; Chandra *et al.*, 2017; Enioutina *et al.*, 2017; Timbreza *et al.*, 2017; Bate *et al.*, 2020).

Lichens are classic examples for mutualistic interaction between a photosynthetic partner designated as photobiont (an alga or a cyanobacterium) and a fungal partner designated as mycobiont. Lichens are ubiquitous and occur in almost all climatic conditions. The growth forms of lichens are crustose, squamulose, foliose and fructicose (Shukla *et al.*, 2010; Seminara *et al.*, 2018; Kekuda *et al.*, 2019; Nunes *et al.*, 2019). Lichens are known to have medicinal, ritual and spiritual values. Lichens are traditionally used as a source of food, spice, dye and perfumes. Lichens have been used in traditional medicine all over the world. Ailments or diseases such as are treated using several lichen species (Upreti *et al.*, 2005; Shukla *et al.*, 2014; Singh *et al.*, 2015; Devkota *et al.*, 2017; Rajeswari *et al.*, 2019). Lichens are resources of a variety of secondary metabolites (lichen substances), most of which are specific to lichens and do not occur in other organisms. Crude extracts and purified metabolites from lichens have been investigated for various bioactivities. It has been shown that lichens exhibit various pharmacological activities such as antimicrobial, anti-inflammatory, antioxidant, anti-inflammatory, insecticidal, cytotoxic, herbicidal and enzyme inhibitory activities (Pereira *et al.*, 2010; Kumar *et al.*, 2011; Kekuda *et al.*, 2011; Kekuda *et al.*, 2012; Shivanna and Garampalli, 2015; Moreira *et al.*, 2015; Sachin *et al.*, 2018; Kekuda *et al.*, 2019; Gazo *et al.*, 2019). In this study, we report antibacterial potential of methanolic extract of four fruticose macrolichens against a panel of Gram positive and Gram negative bacteria.

2. Materials and Methods

2.1. Collection and identification of lichens

The macrolichens selected for this study were collected at Hosagunda, Shivamogga district, Karnataka during December 2018. Identification of the lichens was done by morphological, anatomical and color tests. Secondary metabolites were detected by Thin Layer Chromatography (TLC) (Awasthi, 2007; Culberson and Kristinsson, 1970; Culberson, 1972).

2.2. Extraction

The collected and powdered lichens were extracted using methanol (HiMedia, Mumbai) by maceration process as described in the study of Ankith *et al.* (2017). The methanolic extracts of lichens were prepared in dimethyl sulfoxide (DMSO; HiMedia, Mumbai) and tested for antibacterial activity.

2.3. Antibacterial activity of lichen extracts

2.3.1. Test bacteria

Two Gram positive bacteria *viz.*, *Staphylococcus aureus* and *Bacillus cereus* and three Gram negative bacteria viz. *Salmonella typhi*, *Pseudomonas aeruginosa* and *Escherichia coli* were used.

2.3.2. Antibacterial assay

In vitro antibacterial activity of extracts of selected lichens (20 mg extract/ml of DMSO) was evaluated by Agar well diffusion assay as described in the study of Kambar *et al.* (2014). Streptomycin (1 mg/ml of sterile distilled water) was used as positive control and DMSO was used as negative control. Zones of inhibition (ZOI) were measured using a ruler.

3. Results and Discussion

Details on the result of the yield of extract obtained, color tests and secondary metabolites detected by TLC is shown in Table - 1. The yield obtained was highest in case of *R. conduplicans* and least in case of *R. nervulosa*.

Agar well diffusion method is one of the routinely used in vitro antibacterial assays and is used to evaluate antibacterial potential of several lichen extracts (Devi *et al.*, 2011; Baral and Maharjan, 2011; Chauhan and Abraham, 2013; Kambar *et al.*, 2014; Vinayaka *et al.*, 2017; Plaza *et al.*, 2018). The result of antibacterial potential of selected macrolichens is presented in Table - 2. All lichens were effective in causing inhibition of test bacteria. Among test bacteria, marked susceptibility to lichen

extracts was noticed in case of Gram positive bacteria than Gram negative bacteria. Overall, extract of *R. conduplicans* displayed stronger antibacterial potential when compared to other lichen extracts. *B. subtilis* and *E. coli* were inhibited to highest extent among Gram positive and Gram negative bacteria, respectively. Reference antibiotic caused inhibition of test bacteria to more extent when compared to lichen extracts. The negative control DMSO showed no inhibitory activity against any of the test bacteria. In similar studies, antibacterial activities of *R. conduplicans* (Kambar *et al.*, 2014; Ankith *et al.*, 2017), and *R. nervulosa* (Sundararaj *et al.*, 2015; Gazo *et al.*, 2019), have been reported.

Table - 1: Yield, color test and TLC of lichens selected for this study

Lichen	Family	Color test	Secondary metabolites	Extract yield (%)
U. aciculifera	Parmeliaceae	Medulla K+ yellow, C-, P+ yellow	Usnic acid, stictic acid, constictic acid	8.96
R. conduplicans	Ramalinaceae	Cortex K-, Medulla K-, C-, KC-, Pd+ yellow	Usnic acid, Salazinic acid, Sekikaic acid	9.98
R. nervulosa	Ramalinaceae	C -, P -, K+ pink or K -	Sekikaic acid, Usnic acid	8.36
T. flavicans	Teloschistaceae	K+ purple, C-, KC-, P-	Parietin	8.65

Table - 2: Inhibition of test bacteria by lichen extracts

Lichen	ZOI (cm)				
	S. aureus	*B. subtilis*	*E. coli*	*S. typhi*	*P. aeruginosa*
U. aciculifera	2.40±0.00	2.50±0.00	2.23±0.05	1.70±0.10	2.13±0.05
R. nervulosa	2.53±0.00	3.10±0.10	2.40±0.00	2.30±0.10	2.20±0.00
R. conduplicans	2.96±0.05	3.23±0.05	2.73±0.05	2.40±0.00	2.30±0.00
T. flavicans	2.50±0.00	2.90±0.00	2.30±0.00	1.83±0.05	1.70±0.10
Antibiotic	4.06±0.05	4.10±0.00	3.20±0.00	2.80±0.00	3.13±0.05
DMSO	0.00±0.00	0.00±0.00	0.00±0.00	0.00±0.00	0.00±0.00

4. Conclusion

The lichens selected in this study were effective against Gram positive and Gram negative bacteria. These lichens may be used as natural agents to treat infectious bacterial diseases. The secondary metabolites identified in the lichens might have been responsible for the observed inhibitory potential.

5. References

1) Ankith GN, Rajesh MR, Karthik KN, Avinash HC, Kekuda PTR, Vinayaka KS. Antibacterial and antifungal activity of three *Ramalina* species. Journal of Drug Delivery and Therapeutics 2017; 7(5): 27-32.

2) Aslam B, Wang W, Arshad MI, Khurshid M, Muzammil S, Rasool MH, Nisar MA, Alvi RF, Aslam MA, Qamar MU, Salamat MKF, Baloch Z. Antibiotic resistance: a rundown of a global crisis. Infection and Drug Resistance 2018; 11: 1645-1658.

3) Awasthi DD. A compendium of the macrolichens from India, Nepal and Sri Lanka, Bishen Singh Mahendra Pal Singh, Dehra Dun, India, 2007.

4) Baral B, Maharjan BL. Assessment of antimicrobial and phytochemical potentials of high altitudinal Nepalese lichens. Journal of Microbiology, Biotechnology and Food Sciences 2011; 1(2): 98-112.

5) Basappa K, Venu Gopal J. Natural alternatives to antibiotic agents. Asian Journal of Biomedical and Pharmaceutical Sciences 2013; 3(24): 1-4.

6) Bate PNN, Orock AE, Nyongbela KD, Babiaka SB, Kukwah A, Ngemenya MN. In vitro activity against multi-drug resistant bacteria and cytotoxicity of lichens collected from Mount Cameroon. Journal of King Saud University – Science 2020; 32(1): 614–619.

7) Chandra H, Bishnoi P, Yadav A, Patni B, Mishra AP, Nautiyal AR. Antimicrobial resistance and the alternative resources with special emphasis on plant-based antimicrobials - A review. Plants 2017; 6: 16.

8) Chauhan R, Abraham J. *In vitro* antimicrobial potential of the lichen *Parmotrema* sp. extracts against various pathogens. Iranian Journal of Basic Medical Science 2013; 16(7): 882-885.

9) Culberson CF, Kristinsson H. A standardized method for the identification of lichen products. Journal of Chromatography 1970, 46, 85-93.

10) Culberson CF. Improved conditions and new data for the identification of lichen products by a standardized thin layer chromatographic method. Journal of Chromatography 1972; 72: 113-125.

11) Devi KG, Anantharaman P, Kathiresan K, Balasubramanian T. Antimicrobial activities of the lichen *Roccella belangeriana* (Awasthi) from mangroves of Gulf of Mannar. Indian Journal of Geo-Marine Sciences 2011; 40(3): 449-453.

12) Devkota S, Chaudhary RP, Werth S, Scheidegger C. Indigenous knowledge and use of lichens by the lichenophilic communities of the Nepal Himalaya. Journal of Ethnobiology and Ethnomedicine 2017; 13(1): 15.

13) Enioutina EY, Teng L, Fateeva TV, Brown JCS, Job KM, Bortnikova VV, Krepkova LV, Gubarev MI, Sherwin CMT. Phytotherapy as an alternative to conventional antimicrobials: combating microbial resistance. Expert Review of Clinical Pharmacology 2017; 10(11): 1203-1214.

14) Gazo SMT, Santiago KAA, Tjitrosoedirjo SS, Cruz TEED. Antimicrobial and herbicidal activities of the fruticose lichen *Ramalina* from Guimaras Island, Philippines. Biotropia 2019; 26(1): 23-32.

15) Kambar Y, Vivek MN, Manasa M, Kekuda PTR, Onkarappa R. Antimicrobial activity of *Ramalina conduplicans* Vain. (Ramalinaceae). Science, Technology and Arts Research Journal 2014; 3(3): 57-62.

16) Kekuda PTR, Lavanya D, Pooja R, Lichens as promising resources of enzyme inhibitors: A review. Journal of Drug Delivery and Therapeutics 2019; 9(2-s):665-676.

17) Kekuda PTR, Raghavendra HL, Swathi D, Venugopal TM, Vinayaka KS. Antifungal and cytotoxic activity of *Everniastrum cirrhatum* (Fr.) Hale. Chiang Mai Journal of Science 2012; 39(1): 76-83.

18) Kekuda PTR, Vinayaka KS, Swathi D, Suchitha Y, Venugopal TM, Mallikarjun N. Mineral composition, total phenol content and antioxidant activity of a macrolichen *Everniastrum cirrhatum* (Fr.) Hale (Parmeliaceae). E-Journal of Chemistry 2011; 8(4): 1886-1894.

19) Kumar AHS, Kekuda PTR, Vinayaka KS, Swathi D, Venugopal TM. Anti-obesity (Pancreatic lipase inhibitory) activity of *Everniastrum cirrhatum* (Fr.) Hale (Parmeliaceae). Pharmacognosy Journal 2011; 3(19): 65-68.

20) Kumar SG, Adithan C, Harish BN, Sujatha S, Roy G, Malini A. Antimicrobial resistance in India: A review. Journal of Natural Science, Biology and Medicine 2013; 4(2): 286-291.

21) Manchanda V, Sanchaita S, Singh N. Multidrug resistant *Acinetobacter*. Journal of Global Infectious Diseases 2010; 2(3): 291-304.

22) Moreira AS, Braz-Filho R, Mussi-Dias V, Vieira IJ. Chemistry and biological activity of *Ramalina* lichenized fungi. Molecules 2015; 20(5): 8952-8987.

23) Nunes L, Burle G, Gumboski EL, Dechoum M. Abiotic effects on the cover and richness of corticolous lichens on *Araucaria angustifolia* trunks. Acta Botanica Brasilica 2019; 33(1): 21-28.

24) Pereira EC, da Silva NH, Santos RA, Sudario APP, Silva AAR, Maia MBS. Determination of *Teloschistes flavicans* (sw) norm anti-inflammatory activity. Pharmacognosy Research 2010; 2(4): 205-210.

25) Plaza CM, de Salazar CP, Plaza RE, Vizcaya M, Rodriguez-Castillo G, Medina-Romirez G. *In vitro* analysis of antibacterial and antifungal potential of lichen species of *Everniastrum vexans, Parmotrema blanquetianum, Parmotrema reticulatum* and *Peltigera laciniata*. MOJ Drug Design Development and Therapy 2018; 2(3): 125-134.

26) Rajeswari N, Mesta AR, Vinayaka KS, Babu RHN. Medicinal importance of Usneoid lichens in Western Ghats, southern India. Plant Archives 2019; 19(2): 2540-2542.

27) Reygaert WC. An overview of the antimicrobial resistance mechanisms of bacteria. AIMS Microbiology 2018; 4(3): 482-501.

28) Sachin MB, Mahalakshmi SN, Kekuda PTR. Insecticidal efficacy of lichens and their metabolites—A mini review. Journal of Applied Pharmaceutical Science 2018; 8(10): 159-164.

29) Seminara A, Fritz J, Brenner MP, Pringle A. A universal growth limit for circular lichens. Journal of the Royal Society Interface 2018; 15(143): 20180063.

30) Shivanna R, Garampalli RH. Evaluation of fungistatic potential of lichen extracts against *Fusarium solani* (Mart.) Sacc. causing Rhizome rot disease in Ginger. Journal of Applied Pharmaceutical Science 2015; 5(10): 67-72.

31) Shukla P, Upreti DK, Nayaka S, Tiwari P. Natural dyes from Himalayan lichens. Indian Journal of Traditional Knowledge 2014; 13(1): 195-201.

32) Shukla V, Joshi GP, Rawat MSM. Lichens as a potential natural source of bioactive compounds: a review. Phytochemistry Reviews 2010; 9: 303–314.

33) Singh S, Upreti DK, Lehri A, Paliwal AK. Quantification of lichens commercially used in traditional perfumery industries of Uttar Pradesh, India. Indian Journal of Plant Sciences 2015; 4(1):29-33.

34) Sundararaj JP, Kuppuraj S, Ganesan A, Ponnusamy P, Nayaka S. In vitro assesssment of antioxidant and antimicrobial activities of different solvent extracts from lichen *Ramalina nervulosa*. International Journal of Pharmacy and Pharmaceutical Sciences 2015; 7(8): 200-204.

35) Timbreza LP, Reyes JLD, Flores CHC, Perez RHLA, Stockel MAS, Santiago KAA. Antibacterial activities of the lichen *Ramalina* and *Usnea* collected from Mt. Banoi, Batangas and Dahilayan, Bukidnon, against multi-drug resistant (MDR) bacteria. Austrian Journal of Mycology 2017; 26: 27-42.

36) Upreti DK, Divakar PK, Nayaka S. Commercial and ethnic use of lichens in India. Economic Botany 2005; 59: 269.

37) Vinayaka KS, Kekuda PTR, Kumar PSK. Antimicrobial activity of *Coccocarpia erythroxyli* (Spreng.) swinc. & krog. Journal of Pharmacognosy and Phytochemistry 2017; 6(6): 2419-2422.

Nature and Medicine: Traditional Uses, Chemistry and Bioprocessing of Natural Products
ISBN: 978-81-947154-3-6
First Edition; 2020
Chapter – 12, Page: 120 - 133

12

STUDIES ON ANTIFUNGAL, ANTIOXIDANT AND INSECTICIDAL ACTIVITIES OF *Phyllodium pulchellum* (L.) Desv.

Supriya H.S[1], Yashaswini S.L[1], Supreetha G[1], Umme Farda Khanum[1], Prashith Kekuda T.R[1*] and Raghavendra H.L[2]

[1]Department of Microbiology, S.R.N.M.N College of Applied Sciences, NES Campus, Balraj Urs road, Shivamogga – 577 201, Karnataka, India
[2]Faculty of Medicine, The Medical School (FMB), Sao Paulo State University (UNESP), Botucatu-18618-687, Sao Paulo State, Brazil.
*Corresponding author: p.kekuda@gmail.com

Abstract

In this study, we report antifungal, antioxidant and insecticidal properties of leaves of *Phyllodium pulchellum* (L.) Desv. (Leguminosae). Preliminary phytochemical analysis of methanolic extract of leaves identified alkaloids, flavonoids, tannins, saponins, triterpenes and glycosides. Antifungal activity as evaluated by poisoned food technique revealed the potential of leaf extract to inhibit *Aspergillus niger* to higher extent than *A. flavus*. The leaf extract scavenged DPPH and ABTS radicals dose dependently with an IC_{50} value of 21.3 µg/ml and 18.3 µg/ml respectively. The extract also exhibited ferric reducing efficacy. Insecticidal activity as screened by larvicidal assay highlighted the potential of leaf extract to cause mortality (60 %) of II instar larvae of *Anopheles* species. The leaves of *P. pulchellum* can be used to prevent or manage fungal diseases, oxidative damage and mosquito-borne diseases.

Key words: *Phyllodium pulchellum*, Maceration, Poisoned food technique, DPPH, Ferric reducing and Insecticidal activity.

1. Introduction

Plants have been exploited by humans for various needs such as food, shelter, cloth, fuel and medicine since time immemorial. People especially living in remote places rely on medicinal plants to meet primary healthcare. Indigenous systems of medicine such as Ayurveda, Siddha, Unani and Traditional Chinese Medicine use a large number of plant species to treat several ailments. Plants are used either singly or in certain combinations or formulations to treat several diseases including cancer. Plant based medicines are gaining popularity these days due to their local availability, no or least side effects besides low cost. The therapeutic potential of plants is attributed to the presence of secondary metabolites such as polyphenolic compounds, alkaloids and terpenes. Most of the modern drugs have got their origin in traditional medicine. Compounds such as vincristine, vinblastine, taxol, quinine, morphine, and nicotine have their origin in plants (Cowan, 1999; Fabricant and Farnsworth, 2001; Patwardhan, 2005; Mukherjee *et al.*, 2007; Ravishankar and Shukla, 2007; Raghavendra *et al.*, 2017; Raj *et al.*, 2018).

Phyllodium pulchellum (L.) Desv. [Syn: *Desmodium pulchellum* (L.) Benth], a shrub belonging to the family Leguminosae can grow up to 2m in height. The plant is characterized by grey-pubescent branches, trifoliate leaves, racemose inflorescence with fascicles of flowers in the axils of conspicuous foliar bracts (Bhat, 2014). *P. pulchellum* is used in several countries for various ethnobotanical purposes. The plant is used as fodder, forage and edible plant (Dangol, 2002; Khumgratok *et al.*, 2005) and is traditionally used as insect repellant, for preparation of rice beer, to ease delivery, as a cure for cancer, hemorrhages, fever, edema, liver injury and viral infections (Chuakul *et al.*, 2002; Deori *et al.*, 2007; Obico and Ragragio, 2014; Khuankaew *et al.*, 2014; Agnihotri *et al.*, 2016; Kusum *et al.*, 2016; Zhao *et al.*, 2019; Ren *et al.*, 2019).

The plant *P. pulchellum* is reported to exhibit antidiabetic (Noor *et al.*, 2013), hepatoprotective (Fan *et al.*, 2018), anti-inflammatory (Noor *et al.*, 2013), anti-proliferative (Wang *et al.*, 2014), Antinociceptive (Ahmed *et al.*, 2013), antidepressant (Chitcharoenthum and Theramongkol, 1990), anthelmintic (Chitcharoenthum *et al.*, 1989), antibacterial (Velmurugan and Anand, 2016), antifungal (Velmurugan and Anand, 2017a), antioxidant (Velmurugan and Anand, 2017b), and antidiarrheal activities (Rahman *et al.*, 2013). In the present study, we screened the leaf extract of *P. pulchellum* for antifungal, antioxidant and insecticidal activities.

Chapter - 11

2. Materials and Methods

2.1. Collection, extraction and phytochemical analysis

P. pulchellum was collected at Haniya, Hosanagara, Shivamogga during December 2019, authenticated by Dr. Vinayaka K.S, Assistant Professor and head, Dept. of Botany, SVS College, Bantwal. The leaf powder was extracted using methanol by maceration process by following the protocol of Raghavendra *et al.* (2017). The color and yield of extract was noted. The leaf extract was screened for the presence of phytochemicals such as alkaloids, flavonoids, tannins, saponins, triterpenoids and glycosides by Standard phytochemical analyses (Doss, 2009; Rao *et al.*, 2016; Gul *et al.*, 2017).

2.2. Antifungal activity of leaf extract

Antifungal property of leaf extract (1mg extract/ml of potato dextrose agar medium) was determined by poisoned food technique as described in the study of (Raghavendra *et al.*, 2017). The extent of inhibition of fungal growth in poisoned plates was calculated.

2.3. Antioxidant activity of leaf extract

2.3.1. DPPH (2,2-diphenyl-1-pricryl hydrazyl) radical scavenging assay

Various concentrations (6.25 - 200 µg/ml of methanol) of leaf extract and ascorbic acid (standard) was screened for their antiradical property by DPPH assay as described in the study of Raghavendra *et al.* (2017). IC_{50} value for leaf extract and ascorbic acid was calculated.

2.3.2. ABTS (2,2′-azino-bis-3-ethylbenzthiazoline-6-sulfonic acid) radical scavenging assay

The antiradical potential of different concentrations (6.25-200 µg/ml of methanol) of leaf extract and ascorbic acid (standard) was also evaluated by ABTS radical scavenging assay as described in the study of Raghavendra *et al.* (2017). IC_{50} value for leaf extract and ascorbic acid was calculated.

2.3.3. Ferric reducing assay

The reducing potential of leaf extract was determined by reducing power assay as described in the study of Pavithra *et al.* (2013). Ascorbic acid was used as reference standard.

2.4. Insecticidal activity of leaf extract

Second instar larvae of *Anopheles* species were tested for their susceptibility to leaf extract (1 mg/ml of water). Insecticidal potential of leaf extract was tested in terms of its larvicidal potential by following the protocol of Raghavendra *et al.* (2017). DDT (0.1 %) was used as reference standard. DMSO was used as negative control.

3. Results and Discussion

3.1. Yield of leaf extract

Extraction is the first step to separate the bioactive compounds from the plant materials. In the present study, we employed Maceration process for extraction of the plant material. Maceration is a very simple extraction protocol being extensively used in phytochemistry for the extraction of thermolabile components (Zhang *et al.*, 2018). Methanol was selected as solvent for extraction of plant materials in our study, as methanol is polar and is shown to dissolve most of the bioactive compounds such as polyphenolic compounds, terpenoids, saponins and tannins (Cowan, 1999; Zhang *et al.*, 2018). Details on colour and yield of extract obtained was shown in Table - 1. The yield of extract was 10.77 % and the color of leaf extract was brownish orange. Table - 2 shows different phytochemicals identified in the leaf extract of *P. pulchellum*. The leaf extract was shown to contain alkaloids, flavonoids, tannins, saponins, glycosides, triterpenoids and steroids. The study of Velmurugan and Anand (2016) also showed the presence of these phytoconstituents in the leaves of *P. pulchellum*.

Table - 1: Colour and yield of the leaf extract

Parameter	*P. pulchellum*
Quantity of powder	10 g
W2 (weighing dish + leaf extract)	69.980 g
W1 (weighing dish only)	68.903 g
Weight of extract (w2-w1)	1.077 g
Yield of extract (%)	10.77 %
Colour of extract	Brownish orange

Table - 2: Phytoconstituents detected in the leaf extract

Phytochemical	Leaf extract
Alkaloids	+
Flavonoids	+
Tannins	+
Saponins	+
Steroids	+
Glycosides	+
Triterpenoids	+

Chapter - 11

3.2. Antifungal activity of leaf extract

Botanicals have shown to be effective alternatives for fungicides of synthetic origin and many studies on the solvent extracts and isolated compounds from higher plants exhibit antifungal activity against many phytopathogenic fungi including seed-borne fungi (Lindsey and van Staden, 2004; Tapwal *et al.*, 2011; Bajpai and Kang, 2012; Kambar *et al.*, 2014; Ayesha *et al.*, 2018). Table - 3 and Figure - 1 shows the antifungal effect of leaf extract of *P. pulchellum*. Among the fungi, marked susceptibility to extract was recorded in case of *Aspergillus niger* (48.88 % inhibition) than *A. flavus* (35.89 %). In addition to suppression of hyphal growth, the sporulation was also affected. In an earlier study, Velmurugan and Anand (2017a) showed the dose dependent antifungal efficacy of chloroform and ethanol extracts of *P. pulchellum* leaves against *A. niger* and other fungi.

Table - 3: Growth of test fungi in control and poisoned plates

Treatment	Colony diameter (cm)	
	A. niger	*A. flavus*
Control	4.5	3.9
Leaf extract	2.3	2.5

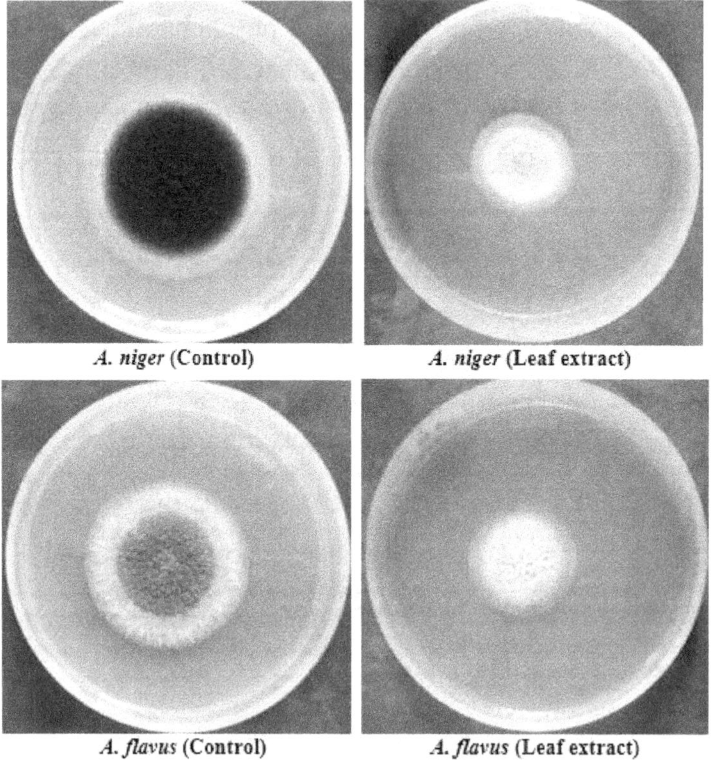

Figure - 1: Growth of test fungi in control and poisoned plates

3.3. Antioxidant activity of leaf extract

3.3.1. DPPH scavenging activity of leaf extract

DPPH free radical scavenging assay is one of the most popular *in vitro* antiradical assays wherein the samples with hydrogen donating potential will scavenge DPPH radicals (purple) and convert them into DPPHH (yellow; diphenylpicryl hydrazine). DPPH assay is extensively used to evaluate antiradical activity of plants (Chung *et al.*, 2006; Elmastas *et al.*, 2006; Sajeesh *et al.*, 2011; Sowndhararajan and Kang, 2013). The leaf extract as well as ascorbic acid were effective in producing dose dependent scavenging of DPPH radicals. However, ascorbic acid scavenged DPPH radicals more efficiently (IC_{50} 6.28 µg/ml) than leaf extract (IC_{50} 21.3 µg/ml). A scavenging activity of 50 % and higher was observed at concentration 25.00 µg/ml and 12.50 µg/ml of leaf extract and ascorbic acid respectively (Figure - 2). The result obtained is in accordance with the study by Velmurugan and Anand (2017c) which showed dose dependent scavenging of DPPH radicals by ethanolic, chloroform and aqueous extracts of leaves of *P. pulchellum*. In a recent study, Fan *et al.* (2018) revealed scavenging potential of two flavonoid compounds viz. (-)-gallocatechin (3) and (-)-epigallocatechin isolated from aerial parts of *P. pulchellum* against DPPH radicals. It is clear that the leaf extract possess hydrogen donating property and may act possibly as primary antioxidant through its free radical scavenging property.

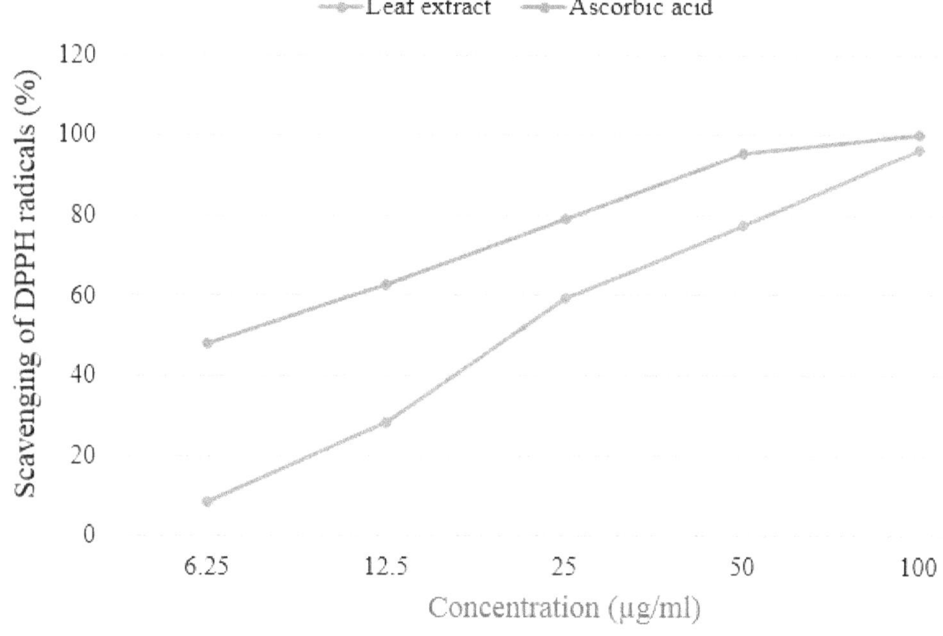

Figure - 2: Extent of scavenging of DPPH radicals by leaf extract

3.3.2. ABTS radical scavenging assay

ABTS radical scavenging assay is another assay used to evaluate radical scavenging potential of various kinds of samples including botanicals. In this assay, the antioxidants either transfer electrons or hydrogen atoms to ABTS radical resulting in neutralization of its free radical character (Ashafa *et al.*, 2010; Rakesh *et al.*, 2013; Raghavendra *et al.*, 2017; Ondua *et al.*, 2019; El Omari *et al.*, 2019). The leaf extract of *P. pulchellum* as well as ascorbic acid displayed dose dependent scavenging activity against ABTS radicals (Figure - 3). The leaf extract scavenged ABTS radicals with an IC_{50} value of 18.3µg/ml and the activity is lower than that of ascorbic acid (IC_{50} value of 5.87 µg/ml). It is shown that the leaf extract possess hydrogen donating potential and hence, it can possibly behave as a primary antioxidant through its free radical scavenging nature.

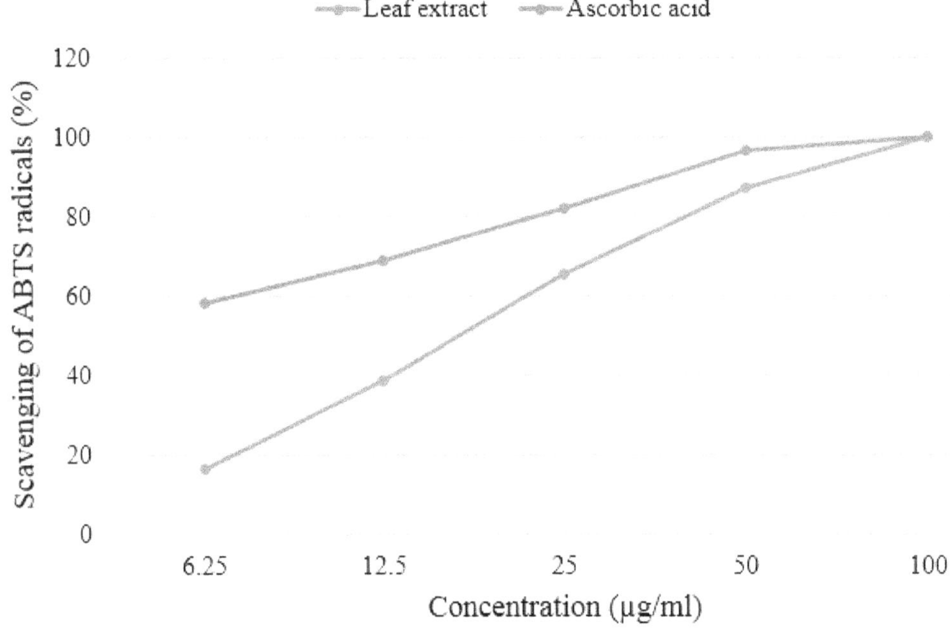

Figure - 3: Extent of scavenging of ABTS radicals by leaf extract

3.3.3. Ferric reducing activity of leaf extract

We performed ferric reducing assay to evaluate reducing property of *P. pulchellum* and measured the extent of reduction of $Fe^{+3}(CN)_6$ to $Fe^{+2}(CN)_6$ at 700 nm. This *in vitro* assay has been widely used to evaluate antioxidant nature of plant extracts (Choi *et al.*, 2007; Pavithra *et al.*, 2013; Bhalodia *et al.*, 2013; Junaid *et al.*, 2013). Figure - 4 shows the reducing capacity of leaf extract of *P. pulchellum*. It was observed that the reducing powers of leaf extract as well as ascorbic acid increased with the increase of their concentrations. It is clear from the result that the leaf

extract of *P. pulchellum* possess reducing potential and serve as electron donor, and thereby breaking the radical chain reactions.

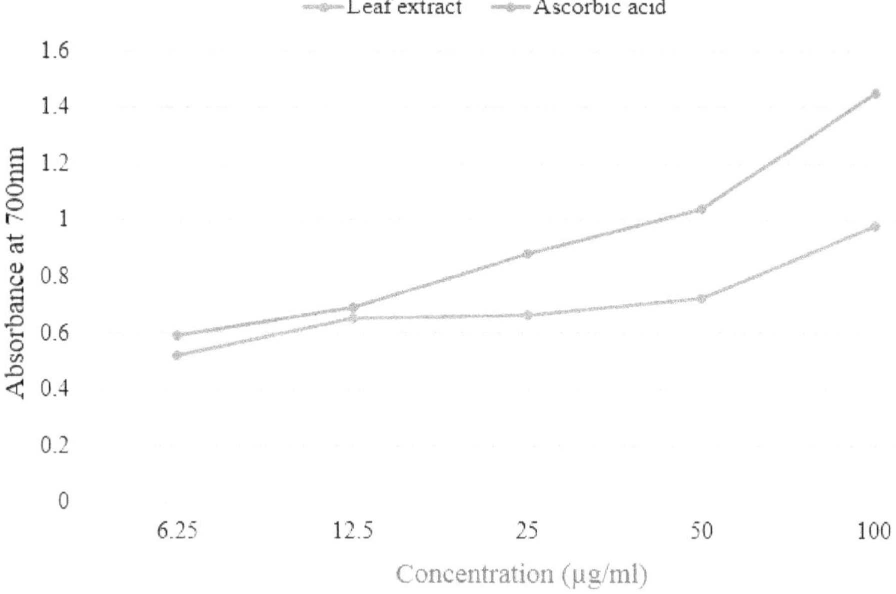

Figure - 4: Ferric reducing activity of leaf extract

3.4. Insecticidal activity of leaf extract

Mosquitoes are important as they are vectors for transmission of several diseases like dengue, chikungunya, and malaria. Targeting the larvae of mosquitoes is the widely used strategy for mosquito control. Solvent extracts as well as purified secondary metabolites from plants to exhibit insecticidal potential (Kovendan *et al.*, 2012; Krishnamoorthy *et al.*, 2015; Govindarajan *et al.*, 2016; Raghavendra *et al.*, 2017; Ramesh *et al.*, 2017). In the present study, the mortality of II instar larvae of *Anopheles* species was recorded after 24 hours of exposure to leaf extract. The results of insecticidal activity of the leaf extract were shown in Table - 4. The extract showed 60 % mortality of larvae at 1 mg/ml concentration. There was no death of larvae treated with DMSO. In presence of DDT, all the larvae were killed (100 % mortality).

Table - 4: Larval mortality by leaf extract

Treatment	Number of larvae	Number of dead larvae	Mortality (%)
DMSO control	10	0	0
Leaf extract	20	12	60
DDT	20	20	100

4. Conclusions

In our study, the leaf extract of *P. pulchellum* showed antifungal, antioxidant and insecticidal activities which might be related to phytochemical content of the extract. The plant may be used to manage seed-borne pathogens, and to prevent mosquito-borne diseases and oxidative damage. Further studies have to be carried out to recover and characterize active components from the leaf extract and subjected for pharmacological properties.

Acknowledgements

Authors express their sincere thanks to HOD, Dept. of Microbiology, Principal, S.R.N.M.N College of Applied Sciences and the Management, N.E.S, Shivamogga for providing facilities and moral support to conduct the work. Authors thank Dr. Vinayaka K.S. for assisting us in collection and identification of the plant material.

5. References

1) Agnihotri P, Katiyar P, Husain T. Ethnobotanically important plants of Kishanpur Wildlife Sanctuary, Uttar Pradesh, India. Pleione 2016; 10(1): 32-42.

2) Ahmed Z, Rahman MS, Alamin GM. Evaluation of antinociceptive activity of ethanolic extract and other fractions of *Desmodium pulchellum* (Fabaceae) bark in mice. Journal of Dhaka International University 2013; 5(2): 126-132.

3) Ashafa AO, Grierson DS, Afolayan AJ. *In vitro* antioxidant activity of extracts from the leaves of *Felicia muricata* thunb. an underutilized medicinal plant in the Eastern Cape Province, South Africa. Afr J Tradit Complement Altern Med. 2010; 7(4): 296-302.

4) Ayesha A, Dhanya Shree VS, Sahana BK, Noorain SGK, Kekuda PTR. Phytochemical screening, antifungal and antioxidant activity of *Strobilanthes heyneana* Nees (Acanthaceae). International Journal of Pharmacy and Biological Sciences 2018; 8(4): 565-572.

5) Bajpai VK, Kang SC. In vitro and in vivo inhibition of plant pathogenic fungi by essential oil and extracts of *Magnolia liliflora* Desr. J Agr Sci Tech. 2012; 14: 845-856.

6) Bhalodia NR, Nariya PB, Acharya RN, Shukla VJ. In vitro antioxidant activity of hydro alcoholic extract from the fruit pulp of *Cassia fistula* Linn. Ayu. 2013; 34(2): 209-214.

7) Bhat GK. Flora of South Kanara (Dakshina Kannada and Udupi districts of Karnataka). Aakriti Prints, Mangalore, India, 2014.

8) Chitcharoenthum M, Tesana S, Kaewkes S. Preliminary study: Effects of *Desmodium pulchellum*'s root on *Opisthorchis viverrini* in hamsters. Srinagarind Medical Journal 1989; 4(3): 190-194.

9) Chitcharoenthum M, Theramongkol P. Behavioral effects of dried methanolic extract from *Desmodium pulchellum* in rats. Srinagarind Hosp Med J. 1990; 5(3): 207-212.

10) Choi Y, Jeong H, Lee J. Antioxidant activity of methanolic extracts from some grains consumed in Korea. Food Chemistry 2007; 103: 130-138.

11) Chuakul W, Saralamp P, Boonpleng A. Medicinal plants used in the Kutchum district, Yasothon Province, Thailand. Thai Journal of Phytopharmacy 2002; 9(1): 22-49.

12) Chung Y, Chien C, Teng K, Chou S. Antioxidative and mutagenic properties of *Zanthoxylum ailanthoides* Sieb & zucc. Food Chemistry 2006; 97: 418-425.

13) Cowan MM. Plant products as antimicrobial agents. Clinical Microbiology Reviews 1999; 12(4): 564-582.

14) Dangol DR. Economic uses of forest plant resources in western Chitwan, Nepal. Banko Janakari 2002; 12(2): 56–64.

15) Deori C, Begum SS, Mao AA. Ethnobotany of Sujen- A local rice beer of Deori tribe of Assam. Indian J Tradit Know. 2007; 6(1): 121-125.

16) Doss A. Preliminary phytochemical screening of some Indian Medicinal Plants. Ancient Science of Life 2009; 29(2): 12-16.

17) El Omari N, Sayah K, Fettach S, El Blidi O, Bouyahya A, Faouzi MEA, Kamal R, Barkiyou M. Evaluation of in vitro antioxidant and antidiabetic activities of *Aristolochia longa* extracts. Evid Based Complement Alternat Med. 2019; 2019: 7384735.

18) Elmastas M, Gulcin I, Isildak O, Kufrevioglu OI, Ibaoglu K, Aboul-Enein HY. Radical scavenging activity and antioxidant capacity of Bay leaf extracts. Journal of Iranian Chemical Society 2006; 3(3): 258-266.

19) Fabricant DS, Farnsworth NR. The value of plants used in traditional medicine for drug discovery. Environ Health Perspect. 2001; 109(suppl 1): 69–75.

20) Fan YC, Yue SJ, Guo ZL, Xin LT, Wang CY, Zhao DL, Guan HS, Wang CY. Phytochemical Composition, Hepatoprotective, and Antioxidant Activities of *Phyllodium pulchellum* (L.) Desv. Molecules 2018; 23(6): 1361.

21) Govindarajan M, Rajeswary M, Hoti SL, Benelli G. Larvicidal potential of carvacrol and terpinen-4-ol from the essential oil of *Origanum vulgare* (Lamiaceae) against *Anopheles stephensi*, *Anopheles subpictus*, *Culex quinquefasciatus* and *Culex tritaeniorhynchus* (Diptera: Culicidae). Res Vet Sci. 2016; 104: 77-82.

22) Gul R, Jan SU, Faridullah S, Sherani S, Jahan N. Preliminary phytochemical screening, quantitative analysis of alkaloids, and antioxidant activity of crude plant extracts from *Ephedra intermedia* indigenous to Balochistan. Sci World J. 2017; 2017: 5873648.

23) Junaid S, Rakesh KN, Dileep N, Poornima G, Kekuda TRP, Mukunda S. Total phenolic content and antioxidant activity of seed extract of *Lagerstroemia speciosa* L. Chemical Science Transactions 2013; 2(1): 75-80.

24) Kambar Y, Manasa M, Vivek MN, Kekuda PTR. Inhibitory effect of some plants of Western Ghats of Karnataka against *Colletotrichum capsici*. Sci Technol Arts Res J. 2014; 3(2): 76-82.

25) Khuankaew S, Srithi K, Tiansawat P, Jampeetong A, Inta A, Wangpakapattanawong P. Ethnobotanical study of medicinal plants used by Tai Yai in Northern Thailand. J Ethnopharmacol. 2014; 151(2): 829-838.

26) Khumgratok S, Wongpakam K, Kanchanamayoon W. Edible plants in cultural forests of northeastern Thailand. Secretariat of the Convention on Biological Diversity. Working together for biodiversity: regional and international initiatives contributing to achieving and measuring progress towards the 2010 target. Abstracts of Poster Presentations at the tenth meeting of the Subsidiary Body on Scientific, Technical and Technological Advice of the Convention on Biological Diversity. Montreal, SCBD, 136 p. (CBD Technical Series no 17), 2005: Pp 73-75.

27) Kovendan K, Murugan K, Shanthakumar SP, Vincent S, Hwang JS. Larvicidal activity of *Morinda citrifolia* L. (Noni) (Family: Rubiaceae) leaf extract against *Anopheles stephensi*, *Culex quinquefasciatus*, and *Aedes aegypti*. Parasitol Res. 2012; 111(4): 1481-1490.

28) Krishnamoorthy S, Chandrasekaran M, Raj GA, Jayaraman M, Venkatesalu V. Identification of chemical constituents and larvicidal activity of essential oil from *Murraya exotica* L. (Rutaceae) against *Aedes aegypti*, *Anopheles stephensi* and *Culex quinquefasciatus* (Diptera: Culicidae). Parasitol Res. 2015; 114(5): 1839-1845.

29) Kusum EM, Priti T, Harishankar P. Traditional use of medicinal plants practiced by the Oraon tribe of Jashpur district, CG, India. Research Journal of Recent Sciences 2016; 5: 36-38.

30) Lindsey KL, van Staden J. Growth inhibition of plant pathogenic fungi by extracts of *Allium sativum* and *Tulbaghia violacea*. South African Journal of Botany 2004; 70(4): 671–673.

31) Mukherjee PK, Rai S, Kumar V, Mukherjee K, Hylands P, Hider R. Plants of Indian origin in drug discovery. Expert Opin Drug Discov. 2007; 2(5): 633-657.

32) Noor S, Rahman ASM, Ahmed Z, Das A, Hossain MM. Evaluation of anti-inflammatory and antidiabetic activity of ethanolic extracts of *Desmodium pulchellum* Benth. (Fabaceae) barks on albino wistar rats. Journal of Applied Pharmaceutical Science 2013; 3(7): 48-51.

33) Obico JJA, Ragragio EM. A survey of plants used as repellents against hematophagous insects by the Ayta people of Porac, Pampanga province, Philippines. Philippine Science Letters 2014; 7(1): 179-186.

34) Ondua M, Njoya EM, Abdalla MA, McGaw LJ. Anti-inflammatory and antioxidant properties of leaf extracts of eleven South African medicinal plants used traditionally to treat inflammation. J Ethnopharmacol. 2019; 234: 27-35.

35) Patwardhan B. Ethnopharmacology and drug discovery. J Ethnopharmacol. 2005; 100(1-2): 50-52.

36) Pavithra GM, Siddiqua S, Naik AS, Kekuda PTR, Vinayaka KS. Antioxidant and antimicrobial activity of flowers of *Wendlandia thyrsoidea, Olea dioica, Lagerstroemia speciosa* and *Bombax malabaricum.* Journal of Applied Pharmaceutical Science 2013; 3(6): 114-120.

37) Raghavendra HL, Kekuda PTR, Pushpavathi D, Shilpa M, Petkar T, Siddiqha A. Antimicrobial, radical scavenging, and insecticidal activity of leaf and flower extracts of *Couroupita guianensis* Aubl. Int J Green Pharm 2017; 11(3): 171-179.

38) Rahman MK, Barua S, Islam MF, Islam MR, Sayeed MA, Parvin MS, Islam ME. Studies on the anti-diarrheal properties of leaf extract of *Desmodium puchellum.* Asian Pac J Trop Biomed. 2013; 3(8): 639-643.

39) Raj AJ, Biswakarma S, Pala NA, Shukla G, Vineeta, Kumar M, Chakravarthy S, Bussmann RW. Indigenous uses of ethnomedicinal plants among forest-dependent communities of Northern Bengal, India. J Ethnobiol Ethnomed. 2018; 14: 8.

40) Rakesh KN, Dileep N, Junaid S, Kekuda PTR, Kumar RKA, Vinayaka KS, Raghavendra HL. Elemental analysis (ICP-OES), antibacterial and antioxidant activity of *Maesa indica* (Roxb.) A.DC. Indian Journal of Novel Drug delivery 2014; 6(1): 51-58.

41) Ramesh V, Vijayakumar S, Manogar P, Mahadevan S, Prabhu S and Murugan R. Mosquito larvicidal and pupicidal activity of *Tephrosia purpurea* Linn. (Family: Fabaceae) and *Bacillus sphaericus* against, dengue vector, *Aedes aegypti.* Pharmacognosy Journal 2017; 9(6): 737-742.

42) Rao MUS, Abdurrazak M, Mohd KS. Phytochemical screening, total flavonoid and phenolic content assays of various solvent extracts of tepal of

Musa paradisiaca. Malaysian Journal of Analytical Sciences 2016; 20(5): 1181-1190.

43) Ravishankar B, Shukla VJ. Indian systems of medicine: a brief profile. Afr J Tradit Complement Altern Med. 2007; 4(3): 319-337.

44) Ren X, Xin L, Zhang M, Zhao Q, Yue S, Chen K, Guo Y, Shao C, Wang C. Hepatoprotective effects of a traditional Chinese medicine formula against carbon tetrachloride-induced hepatotoxicity in vivo and in vitro. Biomedicine and Pharmacology 2019; 117: 109190.

45) Sajeesh T, Arunachalam K, Parimelazhagan T. Antioxidant and antipyretic studies on Pothos scandens L. Asian Pac J Trop Med. 2011; 4(11): 889-899.

46) Sowndhararajan K, Kang SC. Free radical scavenging activity from different extracts of leaves of *Bauhinia vahlii* Wight & Arn. Saudi J Biol Sci. 2013; 20(4): 319-325.

47) Tapwal A, Nisha, Garg S, Gautam N, Kumar R. In vitro antifungal potency of plant extracts against five phytopathogens. Braz Arch Biol Technol. 2011; 54(6): 1093-1098.

48) Velmurugan G, Anand SP. Antifungal activity and quantitative phytochemical analysis of *Phyllodium pulchellum* L. Desv.- An important medicinal plant. International Journal of Current Research in Biosciences and Plant Biology 2017a; 4(8): 67-72.

49) Velmurugan G, Anand SP. In vitro antioxidant activity of *Phyllodium pulchellum* L. Desv - A threatened medicinal plant. Asian J Pharm Clin Res. 2017c; 10(10): 282-285.

50) Velmurugan G, Anand SP. In vitro regeneration of a threatened medicinal plant *Phyllodium pulchellum* L. Desv. International Journal of Botany and Research 2017b; 7(4): 61-68.

51) Velmurugan G, Anand SP. Preliminary phytochemical screening and antibacterial activity of *Phyllodium pulchellum* L. Desv. An important medicinal plant. International Journal of Advanced Research 2016; 4(2): 785-791.

52) Wang C, Zhong M, Zhang BJ, Huo XK, Huang SS, Yu SM, Ma XC. Chemical constituents against hepatic fibrosis from *Phyllodium pulchellum* roots. Zhong Yao Cai. 2014; 37(3): 424-427.

53) Zhang Q, Lin L, Ye W. Techniques for extraction and isolation of natural products: A comprehensive review. Chinese Medicine 2018; 13: 20.

54) Zhao Q, Ren X, Chen M, Yue SJ, Zhang MQ, Chen KX, Guo YW, Shao CL, Wang CY. Effects of traditional Chinese medicine formula Le-Cao-Shi on hepatitis B: *In vivo* and *in vitro* studies. J Ethnopharmacol. 2019; 244: 112132.